BELLY

BELLY

HOW I MADE PEACE WITH FOOD, MY BODY AND MYSELF

EMILY J. JOHNSON

Trigger Warning: This publication contains references to subjects that some readers may find distressing including disordered eating, food restriction and associated behaviours, anorexia nervosa, weight and body-shape references, alcoholism, miscarriage, parental death and binge-eating disorder. Reader discretion is advised.

This is a work of creative nonfiction. The events are portrayed to the best of the author's memory. While all the stories in this book are true, some names and identifying details have been changed to protect the privacy of the people involved.

Cover design: Clare Baggaley

Edited and typeset by: Lisa Edwards

ISBN (ebook): 9781739834739

ISBN (paperback): 9781739834722

Created with Vellum

To the woman who gave me life and then later saved it.
This one's for you, Mum x

PROLOGUE

JANUARY 2020

I've just got out of the bath; the towel is wrapped around me. I like my bath. I can hide this body under all the bubbles and I don't have to see it. I'm weightless in the bath. It's a place I'd rather be. Hidden.

As I dry my body with the towel, I watch the ceiling extractor spin around above me. I can't even bring myself to look down at my body. This fat, useless body.

Fat, useless Emily.

I open the bathroom door juggling my clothes, my phone and the two chocolate wrappers from the bars I've just secretly eaten and as I do, the towel knot holding it up unravels and the towel falls down. Dead ahead is a full-length mirror, the one on the landing wall that I constantly avoid. It captures me in all my nakedness. It's just a woman's body, but I can't see it that way.

It's too late. I catch a glimpse of her.

Why did you have to look? Why didn't you just look away?

Frizzy hair dotted with greys and a wrinkly face. Flabby arms and cellulite legs. Faded silvery lines. Sagging breasts. Big hips and rolls of flesh. A fat belly.

Where has my thin body gone from when I was fourteen?

The one I achieved through starving myself? Wasn't I happier then? I'm forty-eight now, seven stones heavier and it's making me miserable.

How could anyone ever love me looking like *this*?

I don't love me.

I don't even like me.

I fucking hate you, Emily.

Have you ever stood in front of a mirror and hated the reflection staring back? Have you looked away uncomfortably, in disappointment, or worse still, disgust? But not before a voice inside your head told you that you were too fat, too thin, too old, too wrinkled, too ugly, too useless, too weak, too ... anything, but never too wonderful or perfect just as you are. Or maybe sometimes you couldn't even bring yourself to look in a mirror at all.

Me too.

A troll took up residence in my head in my teenage years and has been keeping me company ever since - an unwanted bully and far more damaging than any troll you might find online. This one just wouldn't shut up.

You're so fat, Emily...

You're not thin enough...

You're not good enough...

Fat, useless Emily.

I recently reached the glorious milestone of fifty years old and although I now consider it a privilege to have reached this age, I've spent the best part of thirty-seven years uncomfortable in my own skin and hating the shape of my body. I have also spent the same number of years either thinking about food, talking about it, avoiding it and latterly, bingeing on it.

Food, diets and body image have been an unwelcome

obsession of mine since my early teenage years, coinciding with the beginning of puberty and a period of emotional turbulence. Rather than seeing eating food as a necessary action for survival, it has been the bane of my life. Thoughts of food and diets have often filled my head in some form or another, leaving no room for anything else and it has been exhausting.

Instead of nurturing my body and being grateful for the unseen miracles it carries out every day, I've shouted at my reflection in the mirror since I was a teenager. I've criticised her, told her she was fat and useless, sworn at her – hateful words I wouldn't dare utter to another – all because she didn't live up to what I *thought* she should look like.

In 2018, my personal life was in tatters. My family was being torn apart by serious mental illness. I began to consume massive quantities of food at night in secrecy. After a referral by my doctor to an eating disorder clinic in 2019, I was diagnosed with binge-eating disorder (BED).

BED is different from occasional overeating or the odd second or third helping we sometimes find ourselves having from a buffet. It is a serious mental-health condition that sees its sufferers consuming large amounts of food uncontrollably, often in secret, in a short period of time and usually with a great deal of shame. It's one of the most common eating disorders, yet rarely recognised or spoken of, but if left untreated, it can have serious health consequences.

But I was not born with these disordered thoughts about my body shape or food. I arrived on this Earth happy, content and the perfect version of me. Instead, those thoughts were gathered from years of minor trauma, peer pressure, listening to the opinions of others and a lack of self-love.

At some point during my teens, I fell out of love with myself. It has taken me almost forty years, writing two books and three lots of therapy to get to the root causes and to finally love and accept myself as I am.

In my teens, I starved myself and spiralled into anorexia.

In my twenties, I calorie-counted and distracted myself with marriage and babies.

In my thirties, I loved food, as long as everyone else was eating it.

In my forties, I loathed myself and binged.

In my fifties, I've finally learned to love me.

WEE SPARROW

1972

"Come on over here, sit with Ryan and watch what he's doing."

Mum tried coaxing two-year old me to eat with a small pile of grated apple on a plastic plate, set next to my brother who was two years older than me. Even at four years old, Ryan was a hearty eater and devoured everything Mum set down before him. I watched with interest but barely ate a thing. I picked at food.

I was a poor eater as an infant and it had taken Mum over an hour just to get me to drink 2oz of formula milk, after which I would vomit most of it straight back up. The doctors told Mum I had a "delicate stomach" and I became what one would call a 'fussy eater' as I progressed to solid foods. I barely ate – most of the food got tipped over my hair, or over the side of the high-chair. By the age of two, my appetite hadn't improved.

I grew up in London with my parents and brother. My Sussex-born dad was a musician and it was during a gig in Northern Ireland in the 1960s that he first met my mum and they later married before moving to London.

My mum was born in Belfast to a hardworking Catholic

family. She was a former beauty queen who found herself in a world of photoshoots and glamorous gatherings in the sixties, much to her discomfort. She was just a shy twenty-year-old girl who found accidental fame thanks to her natural beauty and voluptuous curves – and a cousin entering her into a competition.

Mum had a threefold mirror that sat on a small dressing table. As a young child I used to sit on her bed behind her, watching her brush her long golden hair after her bath. I thought she was beautiful, a real-life princess. The three mirrors reflected her natural beauty from every angle.

Mum kept a scrapbook of her modelling photos in an old biscuit tin in the bottom of her wardrobe. My grandparents had put it together. The sticky tape holding the photos in was brittle and worn, but I would sit running my fingers carefully over the black and white pictures of my model mum in her swimwear and stilettos. I wanted to be just like Mum.

I couldn't have chosen a better mum. She has the kindest, most giving heart and has loved me fiercely all my life. When I was a little girl, Mum's lap was my safe haven with her warm arms wrapped around me, hugely comforting. I used to sit on her lap and peek inside her flour-dusted apron that she tied around her waist every day. It was a lucky dip of delights in that apron pocket. I'd never know what I might find in there – wooden pegs, tissues, a stray toy, a wilted daisy I'd picked from the garden for her, or perhaps a stone. 'Wee treasures,' she called my garden gifts.

Sadly, I didn't share that connection with my dad. It was often just Mum, Ryan and me: a family of three. We were a family of four, but dad was a sought-after musician by the mid-seventies and would spend weeks away at a time, touring the world with various artists. So, as a little girl, my mum was everything to me. My whole world.

"My wee sparrow," Mum called me. I was underweight and that caused her concern. She spent most of my early childhood quietly following me around the house with food to ensure I ate something. When I began school and was amongst other children, I seemed to find my appetite and began to gain weight. Mum was relieved.

DINNER'S READY!

1979

"Get that down you, son," Mum encouraged warmly, with a ruffle of Ryan's hair and a wink and a smile for me.

"Thanks, Mum!" we sang in unison, eyes wide, excited for her dinner.

By the age of seven, I'd really found my appetite and boy was it an appetite, especially for Mum's cooking. Two generous plates of rich beef stew sat on the table waiting for Ryan and me, the boiled, floury potatoes piled high in the middle, sending clouds of steam towards the yellowed swirls of the kitchen ceiling. A thick gravy river flowed around the potato mountain and our mouths watered in anticipation of another good feed.

Growing up in the late seventies, there was no messing around with food, at least not in our home. We ate whatever Mum dished up without question or complaint. It was either that or go to bed hungry.

By the time Ryan and I would arrive home from school, the kitchen would be filled with the delicious aroma of homemade bread. A warm wheaten loaf made with buttermilk was waiting for us most days and Mum would serve it with butter and sweet strawberry jam. The bread and a glass of creamy milk filled our empty tummies after school and kept Ryan and I fuelled until dinner time.

Just like many other kids in that era, I would bolt inside straight off my bike at teatime, starving after an afternoon spent playing outside. Mum cooked from scratch each night: hearty Irish stews, roast dinners and homemade pies. True to her Irish heritage, there were always plenty of potatoes on the side.

Dinner was *always* followed by a homemade dessert or cake in our house: rice pudding, made with full cream milk and a dollop of strawberry jam, or chocolate marble cake. Ryan and I would be allowed to sit on the kitchen stools next to Mum and we'd bicker over who got to lick the spoon or mixing bowl. The bowl always yielded far more of the delicious raw cake mixture. Every week, Mum would bake an apple pie too. That was my favourite.

"Emily, would you quit picking at it!" Mum would slap a tea towel across the kitchen bench, exasperated at me, shooing me away like an irritating fly.

The smell of the warm pastry would fill the house and I'd steal pieces of the sugary well-baked bits from around the edge of the pie, unable to resist its sweet crunch, as Mum whipped up custard from tinned powder with hot creamy milk. The pie crust would just about poke out of the bowl, swimming in thick yellow custard.

I would save my modest pocket money and spend it in the local village newsagents on a comic and penny sweets every Saturday morning. Just a few pennies went a long way to filling a little white paper bag with unforgivingly sweet delights in the seventies. I savoured my little bag of treats every week. Now and then on a warm summer's afternoon, if we were lucky, we got to enjoy an ice cream with a heavenly chocolate flake crowning the billowy mounds. I'd eagerly watch the shopkeeper pumping snakes of white ice-cream in ever decreasing circles from the chilled silver dispenser, secretly hoping he would keep going. They were considered a real 'treat.'

DAD
1979

"Why are you wearing that bin bag, Daddy?" I enquired, puzzled at my dad's strange preparations before his daily run.

"It helps me sweat, Emily," he replied, in a matter-of-fact tone.

"But why do you want to sweat?" I was confused.

"Because then I might lose this!" Dad confirmed, smirking at me as he slapped his non-existent belly hidden under the bin-bag cover.

As a young man in his mid-twenties, even before he met my mum, my dad was obsessed with his weight and appearance. As he became a successful musician, he became more determined to 'get into shape' before touring, so would go running every day. Before he left to run each day, he would create holes in the bottom of a black bin bag and wear it like a T-shirt under his clothes, to make him sweat more. Dad believed he would lose more weight that way.

He wanted to look like the rock stars in the seventies: stick-thin and adored by women. Throughout their marriage it had always been the same and no matter what my mum said to him, no amount of reasoning would change his mind. But my dad was already slim like his rock-star idols, he just couldn't see it.

My dad didn't use drugs, but he did drink alcohol: far too much and every night. Dad barely ate, purposely restricting calories to ensure he could drink his daily beer allowance without gaining weight. We *never* sat down and ate food together as a family and Dad didn't eat in front of me. Not once can I remember sitting down with him to eat as a child, both because he was often in the pub around dinner time, or gigging, but also because he *didn't eat.*

During the weeks leading up to a tour, he only permitted himself to eat four bran crackers and two boiled eggs during the day, but he would manage several pints of beer in the pub that night. The restrictive diet made him tired and unwell; his gums began to bleed and his dentist advised him he had early signs of malnutrition – but he didn't care and he didn't listen. Dad was obsessed with his appearance both on and off stage.

My dad was equally absent when home as he was abroad. I can vaguely remember him returning home in between tours, but when he came back, he would be at a session in a recording studio in London or in a pub in a different kind of session.

My dad never played with me. He never read to me or hugged me or tucked me into bed at night. Dad didn't know how to be a father. The parenting role didn't come naturally to him, so when home, he was often hovering on the fringes of our family life, unsure how to engage with us. I remember him standing behind the door in the kitchen when my friend occasionally came to play, almost embarrassed to be seen.

Dad was by nature very shy and he found sitting amongst a small group of people – including his family – uncomfortable, but out with his friends with a pint in front of him, he was the life and soul of the party.

MY SECOND HOME

1980

"Go on ahead and fetch me a wee bar ... and get one for yourself," Granny whispers with a wink, as if this forbidden deed is some great secret between us. She lights another cigarette and idly blows the purple-grey smoke into the air staring into nothingness, waiting for her next dopamine fix.

My grandparents owned the local general store in a village in Northern Ireland. It was the kind of shop that sold everything from cigarettes to household items: food, coal, animal feed, paint and even petrol. Granny had an addictive personality – she loved gambling, chain-smoking and had a terrible sweet tooth. She was so hooked on slot machines at the local bingo hall, Granda installed one upstairs in the back of the shop next to the paint and wallpaper. At least that way, whatever money Granny lost in the slots went straight back into Granda's pocket. No one else could use the slot machine – that was forbidden by law as Granda didn't have a gambling licence, but Granny would sit in the back of the shop on a metal stool, gambling and chain-smoking. As one hand pulled the metal arm on the slot machine down, her other would move the cigarette from her lip to the glass ashtray and back again without so much as a glance.

In between pulls, she'd pump one ten-pence piece in after the other. When she had lost her bag full of change, she'd steal a break and send me off to get her a chocolate bar. I'd sneak downstairs to the shop counter and take a bar of Granny's favourite chocolate and one for me too. Granda knew exactly what I was up to, but he played along and pretended to chase after me for my thievery.

Granda was a gentle man with warm eyes and a heart to match. I remember standing next to him watching as he sliced great legs of pink ham with a yellow crumb crust on a shiny silver meat slicer for his customers, whilst they enjoyed the *craic*. Sometimes, he would offer me a slice to nibble on: its salty soft texture was hard to resist.

Granda knew everyone in the village and everyone knew him – and of course, they made it their business to know me. I was a curiosity: the shy little English girl with blue eyes and brown curls. I had my family's Celtic look, despite my English accent.

My school holidays were spent flying home to Ireland – at least Mum called it our home. We lived in England, yet I felt just as comfortable with my family in Northern Ireland. My dad very rarely joined us on those trips. Mum had four siblings and each was married with children, so my holidays back home were loud and chaotic and filled with love. And food.

One of my favourite jobs as a young child was to go to the local bakery a few doors down on my own and collect the fresh bread every day for Granny, before heading to their shop with her. I couldn't resist the smell of the loaf – a large, warm batch loaf wrapped in a white paper bag – as I carried it home under my arm. There was something quite wonderful about that bread – it tasted so different from the bread we had at home in the supermarket. Mum said it was the soft Irish water that made it so delicious. Whatever it was, it was irresistible and I'd peel small bits from the side of the loaf, thinking no one would notice. But one warm doughy mouthful led to another and by the time I reached Granny's house, just minutes away, there was a hole in the side of the loaf. Granny was never cross at me though.

"You want a wee slice, Emily?" she'd ask, grinning, knowing the answer already. Without waiting for a reply, she'd slice giant wedges of bread for us both and smother them in thick, golden Irish butter.

"Sure, it's not worth eating if you can't taste it, isn't that, right?" she'd declare as she sunk her dentures through a sickening creamy layer of salty deliciousness; it was at least half an inch thick and I'd leave teeth marks in it.

"Come on over here, you wee dote, and give us a while of your *craic*," Granny would half-sing to me with one arm outstretched, ready to pull me into her warm-bosomed embrace, her other arm holding the smouldering cigarette away from me. Mugs of tea and cigarettes in the kitchen were part of life and the half-eaten loaf of bread would sit on the table, alongside the butter dish and a bottle of milk with its silver foil lid. It was never warm enough in my granny's kitchen to need to refrigerate it.

Whenever you go to visit someone's home in Ireland for a cup of tea, it is never *just* a cup of tea; it is a cup of tea and a good feed along with it: a hearty fry up of Irish sausages and potato or soda bread, or both, or maybe a fine spread of sandwiches, cakes and plates of biscuits. My grandparents' home was no exception. We had sausages and soda bread farls for breakfast every day, with runny eggs and bacon on potato bread. And on the side was the fresh loaf and plenty of Irish butter.

Between the shop and Granny's home, food was in constant supply. Granny's cupboards were always filled with fresh cream cakes and sweet delights too.

"Go on ahead and help yourself, Emily." Granny held out a plate loaded with chocolate bars and cakes. "Sure, take another couple, it will do you no harm!" She grinned, encouraging me to take several.

"Thanks, Granny." I beamed. I never turned her food invitations down.

Granny couldn't stop at one cake either – in between the cigarettes, she'd easily eat three fresh-cream cakes, one after the other, followed by a plate of chocolate biscuits and mugs of tea to wash it all down. Pastry was her weakness, especially cream eclairs or "wee buns" as she called them.

After her feast, she would sit at the kitchen table smoking, as she stared out of the window at the fields behind the house, clutching at her chest. "Holy Mother of God, Emily, I have the worst heartburn."

PRINCESS EMILY

1980

One of my fondest childhood memories is of my first Holy Communion. Not because I was receiving the Eucharist for the first time – the symbolic body and blood of Jesus Christ – but because Mum handmade a beautiful full-length Communion dress for me in the weeks leading up to the ceremony. I can still picture the dress, a delicate white-satin gown with little flowers imprinted in the fabric; it almost touched the floor. Every time Mum made alterations to my dress, she would let me try it on and I would stand in front of her full-length mirror in awe.

Mum bought me new white sandals about a month beforehand and they had a small heel. I pleaded with her to let me wear them before the ceremony. I'd never worn heels and I so wanted to feel grown up. She agreed, but only allowed me to wear them in the house to keep them perfectly white and intact before the event. I would clump around the kitchen enjoying the sound my new heels made on the lino floor.

On the day of the ceremony, Mum beamed proudly. "Sure, you look like a wee princess, Emily!"

She had pulled my long hair into a bun on top of my head

and placed a crown of little white silk flowers around it, with what felt like a hundred pins to hold it in place and trap the flyaway curls escaping. She secured a small white veil under the bun and finally, I got to put on the shoes I'd been dreaming about for weeks.

"Now, go on ahead and take a wee look at yourself in the mirror. Sure, aren't you just beautiful?" Mum sang.

I stood in front of Mum's bedroom mirror. I *was* a princess, a little bride-to-be, beautifully innocent at just eight years old. I didn't doubt who I was. I didn't wonder if my arms looked fat or if my belly stood out. Those thoughts were not yet present. I just stood and stared at the image before me with a shy, satisfied smile. I loved my dress, my veil and those wonderful white shoes and I loved my reflection too. Princess Emily.

I floated to my Holy Communion with grace, despite the heavy click-clack of new shoes on the grey London pavements.

"Emily, would you come on over here for a picture, give me a wee smile."

"Cheese!" I beamed, happily.

Click, vroom – the noise of the instant camera captured the moment.

BLOSSOMING

1982

I AM STANDING IN FRONT OF MUM'S FITTED WARDROBE. IT has two full-length mirrors, ceiling to floor. Mum is hanging out washing in the garden.

I have a thin cotton dress on and white socks pulled up to my knees. My hair is long and brown curls fall across my shoulders and down my back. I brush it every day and it makes the curls frizz. My face is framed by wisps of hair.

I'm staring at my face. My two front teeth look big and a little out of place. There is a gap between them. Mum said something about me needing to see the dentist soon, she says maybe I need a brace.

My face looks pale and round, a bit like the moon.

Moon face.

I turn to the side. I can see two little lumps on my chest under my dress. I run my fingers over them, they feel strange, soft little mounds.

My eyes move down, scanning my arms, my legs, my belly.

In August 1982, just after my tenth birthday, my parents decided it was time to leave London. We moved to the south coast of England, to a beautiful home on a lovely large treelined road. I adored the garden in my new home: it was mature and well-established and built over three levels, stone steps taking you down to the lawn below. It was full of magic to me – gnarly old trees filled one corner, perfect for making a den underneath them, and mature dense shrubs camouflaged the boundary fences. Higgledy-piggledy flower beds with stone rockeries lined the steps, each one planted with delicate blooms of every colour imaginable. Someone had filled this garden with their love long before we moved in.

In the middle of the lawn sat one big cherry tree. During spring, it filled with the most beautiful pale blossom that fell and decorated the lawn like pink confetti. I'd spend hours alone playing in the garden, often talking to myself as I made perfume concoctions from the fallen petals. I had no friends, having just moved to the area in the summer holidays and not yet started at my new primary school. I was content in my own company, in a garden wonderland of my own make-believe world.

By the age of eleven, I was still a child whose body was morphing slowly into a young woman and I wasn't ready for it. My breasts began changing, small buds at first, and I was both embarrassed and curious. I shied away from the physical changes that were naturally happening even though a small part of me longed to feel grown-up too.

My first bra was a 28-inch A cup. It was so large, it swam on my chest – I barely had enough breasts to fill the cups but somehow it felt very grown-up to be wearing it.

Little did I know the joy I'd feel thirty years later, pulling my bra off every evening after a long day, a bra that cut into my shoulders and encouraged sweat in places it shouldn't because my A cups were now Ds. Over time, I'd learned the art of unclipping it through my clothes and expertly manoeuvring one strap down and out through one sleeve at a time.

Nevertheless, at eleven years old, I desperately wanted that bra. I wanted to fit in with the other girls at my old primary school, some already nudging into a B cup just before school broke up.

BROKEN HOME

1984

"EMILY, YOUR DAD AND I ... WELL, WE LOVE EACH OTHER very much but ... well ... we don't love each other enough to live together anymore," Mum said gently. "It doesn't mean we don't love you or Ryan – we love you, so much, but sometimes this happens."

I could feel a choking lump in my throat and tears threatening to escape. "But *why* don't you love him? "I pleaded.

"Ach, Emily, it's not that simple, love."

Mum sighed heavily as she brushed the wispy stray curls away from my eyes, her soul heavy with her own heartache and my reaction only adding to the pain she must have felt. "I'm going to send you over to Ireland for a few weeks whilst your dad and I sort some things out, okay? When you get back, we will have a nice new house and you can pick your bedroom. How's that?" She smiled warmly, trying to soften the devastating news for herself and me.

"But Mum, I don't want to go, I want to stay with you!" I cried, as I lay my head across her lap, scooping my arms underneath her knees, afraid to let her go.

"You'll be grand, don't you worry your wee head," Mum soothed as she stroked my hair.

My dad had not been home in a long time, but that was nothing new. I didn't understand what was happening or the reasons for it. I'd heard the word divorce before, I understood its meaning, but it felt like such a final event. And as much as my dad wasn't around a lot of the time, to me he was still part of our family and I didn't want my family to be split up.

I lay on my bed that night, with my teddies and Michael Jackson poster on the wall, crying quietly, bewildered and grieving for what had yet to come and wondering if I was somehow to blame for my parents no longer loving each other enough to live together.

Mum appeared at my door. "I bought you a wee treat, Emily."

She'd heard me crying and had brought a plate of toast for me, hot buttery toast with a generous layer of chocolate spread that had melted into the white bread. Its silky brown sweetness glistened in the soft bedside light. Mum sat on the edge of the bed and smiled as she stroked my curls away from my eyes as she always did. I ate the sweet, delicious toast and felt my mother's warmth and love through her gentle touch.

I had only been at my new secondary school a few months when I had to leave again. With six weeks' worth of schoolwork and my favourite stuffed animal, Ryan and I were put on a plane a couple of weeks later to Ireland, to the bosom of my auntie and uncle for almost two months. But this was no holiday – it was term-time and Ryan and I were expected to do our schoolwork. I didn't mind that so much, it meant I got to stay with mum's younger sister, Maryanne.

Aunty Lamb, as I called her, lived in front of a large, beautiful lake in County Monaghan in Southern Ireland. I'd spent many holidays staying there and it was the kind of magical setting that inspired my dreams of whimsical fairies, giants and mythical mermaids that swam the depths of the cold, dark waters. The house was set on a high hill, overlooking the lake with lush green fields either side.

At the bottom of the hill, the lake lapped against large slate boulders leading to a dense forest of mature pine trees that seemed to spread for miles. The house had a roaring wood fire that my uncle would light daily and I would sit next to it in the lounge staring out at the lake watching the rain sweep across the water if the storms had brought us all inside.

Aunty Lamb was warm and kind and like a second mum to me. She looked just like Mum, only she had a different accent – her Belfast tone softened from her years spent living in the south.

Aunty Lamb's kitchen was my favourite place. Just like Mum, she cooked and baked every day. And just like Granny's kitchen, Aunty Lamb's cupboards were always filled with wee sweet treats too.

Every morning I'd come down to a cooked breakfast: my favourite Irish sausages – always well-done – with crispy bacon, potato bread and soda farls fried in the bacon fat; runny egg yolks and a fresh white loaf smothered in butter to mop it all up.

"Do you want some more, wee pet?" Aunty Lamb gently encouraged a second helping with her heavy frying pan full of spare sausages and soda farls, her spatula loaded and ready to refill my plate. I rarely refused.

Aunty Lamb always cooked too much of everything and I ate every day and night at the table until full. That stuffed-with-warm-food feeling felt comforting. And in-between the breakfasts and dinners were wee buns and biscuits and other sweet treats.

I'd sit in the kitchen doing my schoolwork watching Aunty Lamb sing under her breath as she baked apple pies and wee buns and prepared the night's dinner for me, my brother and my cousins. Her cheeks would flush from the heat of the kitchen and the large windowpanes would steam up from the boiling potatoes meeting the damp spring air outside. Aunty Lamb *always* made sure we were well-fed and she tucked me into bed at night. She made me feel safe and loved during a bewildering time.

Some of my fondest childhood memories are my summers spent in Ireland fishing for pike on the lake with my cousins, or the late-night bus rides to nowhere, just for the *craic* with my Aunty Kathleen, and sliding on tin trays down the fresh snowy fields. But my favourite memories were the Christmases spent with all my big, loving family by the roaring fire, feeling stuffed after yet another big feed.

Despite feeling full, we picked at boxes of mint chocolates and tins of sweets from under the Christmas tree. We all agreed we couldn't possibly eat another thing until the orange chocolate was opened and out from the kitchen came a spread of cheeses, crisps and nuts and all manner of snack foods, with left-over turkey and stuffing sandwiches with pickles and cold sausages wrapped in bacon. We feasted on a never-ending buffet until truly fit to burst as we watched Christmas movies on television. Everyone was so happy and content after those big Christmas feasts. Especially me.

ALL CHANGE

JUNE 1985

Ryan and I returned to England seven weeks later to our new home – the old house had already been sold. We moved into a furnished holiday flat in a large old building. It sat next to a busy roundabout but was set back amongst mature trees that provided a buffer from the constant traffic noise. The flat had a strange damp smell that lingered about the old-fashioned, worn furniture, which was at least a decade old. It didn't smell like my home, the one I had left behind.

There were French doors that opened out onto a small balcony: not wide enough for a chair, but big enough that you could stand and watch the squirrels jumping from tree to tree, undisturbed by the noisy traffic nearby. That was my favourite place – up amongst the canopy of dense foliage of the oak trees, watching the birds and traffic, away from the musty smell and uncertainty of a new, unfamiliar life.

It was a temporary home – four weeks later we moved to another one just a couple of roads away from our old house. To reach it, we had to walk past the long fence that encased my old garden, the one that used to be mine. As I passed by, I'd run my fingers along the fence, hitting ridge after ridge of each fence panel. It was stained deep brown from the creosote Mum had soaked it in the summer before. I could still smell its pungent odour and the scent made me sad. Somebody else was in my garden, playing with my den. Were they looking after it? Did they love it in the same way I did?

Our new home smelt clean and was tastefully decorated. The flat was in a house with a staircase and a large garden with a long, green lawn, mature shrub borders and an old swing. That was my favourite place, sat on the swing in the garden, lost in my own thoughts, watching the butterflies dancing above the purple lilac in full bloom.

The flat also had a new man in it – Mum's new friend, Dave. He stayed over sometimes. He was funny and joked a lot and seemed to make my mum happy. But Dave was nothing like my dad in looks or otherwise. My dad was quiet and unobtrusive, though my perception of him was probably that way because he was absent so much. Dave was very different, he was loud and bold and you could hear his raucous laughter before you saw him coming. He was playful towards Mum and full of innuendo as he'd squeeze her in a bear hug and she'd squirm in embarrassment, laughing as she pulled away.

Dave gave Mum a new lease of life, a different one. I liked him. Dave brought me bags of sweets and took me for rides in his car to see his racehorse friends. He made Mum smile and that made me happy too.

A couple of months later, we moved again, this time to a dilapidated house in need of renovation. Dave moved in with us and began work on the house. For several months it was a building site whilst an extension was built, filled with scaffolding and blue tarps as temporary walls and roof to keep out the rain. My new home had a garden too, somewhere, buried under a cement mixer and piles of stones and planks.

Dad, now back from touring life for good, moved to a bedsit a ten-minute drive from Mum's place, behind a busy high street, filled with kebab shops and pubs.

Since Dave had been on the scene, my dad had become more absent. I'd not seen him since Ryan and I had gone to Ireland - he had been staying on various friends' couches, but once he found a place to live, Mum made us visit him.

Dad shared a house with three other men and it was often full of strangers coming and going. He lived sparsely with no furniture in his room, just a mattress on the floor. There was no lounge – it had been rented out as another bedroom.

My dad never had any food in his cupboards and I never saw him cook or eat. The kitchen and bathroom were shared with the other tenants and at twelve years old, I felt uncomfortable sharing a bathroom with four men. The bathroom lock was broken and I was terrified some strange man, or my stranger of a dad, might walk in and see me sitting on the toilet, or worse naked in the bath. My dad was often out gigging at pubs until late at night. His lifestyle just wasn't conducive for us kids, so I rarely visited.

Conversation didn't come easy between me and Dad. Occasionally he would pick me up after school and take me out for a milkshake at the local burger bar. I'd dread it because it made me uncomfortable but I didn't understand why. We'd sit in awkward silence most of the time, making small talk like two strangers sitting in a dentist's waiting room, politely chatting about the weather to pass the time.

I began to feel uncomfortable around my dad the more my body shape changed. Had he noticed? I had new breasts forming, hips and a bit of a belly. I wasn't his little girl anymore. I wondered if it would change the way he felt about me, if he would still love me.

For some reason, it felt awkward to call him Dad. I struggled so much to even say the word. It had been years since I'd called him my daddy. Somehow, over time it had stopped. I felt a little shy and embarrassed around him, so I didn't say a thing. He was nameless to me. I'm sure he noticed but he never said a word. I loved my dad and no doubt he loved me deeply, but I think we both went out for those silent milkshakes out of a sense of unspoken obligation.

Around the same time, he acquired a new girlfriend, Kerry. She was a little clingy to him and I was jealous of the way he spent time so easily with her. Kerry was divorced and lived with her two young children in a large garden flat. On a Sunday afternoon once a month that should have been spent with Dad, I'd be roped into babysitting her young children whilst they went out together. I was still a child, guarding children I barely knew, just so my dad could take his new flame to the pub all afternoon. They'd return a few hours later, a little drunk.

I started to make excuses to not see him. I didn't want to share my dad with another woman. She wasn't my mum. I was sick of being someone else's babysitter, aiding and abetting Kerry in her plans to steal my dad away from me. But most of all, it hurt to see Dad show his love for her so easily.

I began to resent her bleached hair and cheap perfume; the way she threw her head back with exaggerated enthusiasm, laughing at everything my dad said, amusing or not. It annoyed me. Kerry was a lovely woman really and nothing but kind to me, but I was a jealous kid who craved her dad's attention.

My own dad became even more of a stranger to me. Our contact dwindled, he didn't really try and neither did I.

Not long after my parents' divorce completed and Dave had moved in, Dad ended his relationship with Kerry. I was secretly pleased until he announced he was moving away. Dad's heart was still broken from his marriage ending and no woman, not even Kerry, could mend it for him. So, he walked away from us all.

Dad moved back to London and from that point, contact gradually stopped and was reserved to just birthdays and Christmas and the occasional phone call.

A NEW DAD

AUGUST 1985

I AM STANDING IN FRONT OF MUM'S FULL-LENGTH MIRROR. It's on a stand and you can swivel it to change the angle. When I twist around just enough, I can see my backside in it.

I have my school uniform shirt on with navy skirt and white socks pulled up to my knees. My hair is long and in a ponytail. My chestnut curls fall down my back. I tie it up most days now as the frizz gets on my nerves. The wisps of brown curls are no longer wild; they are held down flat with hairspray.

I stand there staring at my face. My two front teeth look different. I am wearing a metal brace. My face looks so round.

I turn to the side. I can see my bra though my white shirt and my breasts stick out. So does my belly and backside. I hate these wide hips. My legs look chunky. I don't look slim, like the models in magazines.

You look fat, Emily.

I pull my skirt up to get a better look at my fat legs. Something catches my eye. Dark red lines run across the inside of both of my thighs.

Oh no, am I going to die?

By the age of thirteen I had gained quite a bit of weight. Mum called it "puppy fat". It was noticeable to me: my face had filled out, as had the rest of my body. As for the strange red marks appearing on the inside of my thighs – I had no idea what they were. I thought I had some deadly disease and ran to Mum for confirmation that I would soon die.

"What's *wrong* with me?" I pleaded as I hitched up my school skirt and showed her the dark lines.

"Emily, love, they're just stretch marks. It's quite normal to get these when you are growing up. They will fade soon and you won't even see them," she soothed.

But soon the stretch marks began to spread. Now they were on the outside of my hips too. They started as a dark shade of purply red, like I'd taken a marker pen to my body. But just as Mum said, they faded to silvery iridescent marks over time. It took a long time, but I kept them hidden as best I could during school sports. They were my little secret.

Mum had been living with Dave for some time when they decided to get married. Dave was a builder by trade, though he was a man of many means. If something was needed, he somehow found a way to acquire it. Mum told me that he got things from some man, "off the back of a lorry".

Once Dave had finished renovating the house, Mum planned their wedding. It was a small affair, a registry office ceremony one Friday afternoon. Mum looked beautiful in her simple summery outfit, a pastel-pink floral dress fashionable for the late eighties, and she plaited her long hair herself, weaving silken flowers through it.

Mum's second marriage thrust me into a new extended family – Dave had two grown-up children so their marriage gifted me a stepbrother in his early twenties and a stepsister who was already married with one child and another on the way.

Dave was a hearty eater and unlike my dad, would sit down three times a day to a meal prepared by Mum. The dining table was regularly scattered with empty dishes and the daily newspapers. Dave would sit there drinking his tea, mug in one hand and a horse-racing fixture book in the other, studying the form. If I caught his eye, he'd wink at me cheerfully.

"Here, Emily – run up the baker's and get us a lardy cake, will you?" He'd rifle through the top pockets of his jacket for loose change. I'd always oblige. Dave had stepped in as my new dad and I wanted to please him.

The local bakery at the top of our road had been there for over forty years. It was one of those old traditional family shops that still had the wind-down red fabric canopy, though it was a little faded and worn at the edges. Its window was filled with batch loaves and cream cakes and daredevil wasps that hovered above the iced buns in the summer, along with lazy flies. The ladies serving wore matching red and white aprons and white paper hats, more for show than cleanliness.

I'd go most Saturdays for Dave's lardy cake, a sweet doughy bread made with lard and sugar and filled with spiced fruit. I'd pick at the sticky fruit from the top of the bread before pushing it back down into the white paper bag as I walked home, the sweet sugary stickiness my reward for running his errand. That and his smile as he shared his lardy cake with me whilst he slurped his mug of tea.

But after a few months of marriage, Dave's charm started to wane. His fondness for racehorses and the acquaintances who owned them had grown. After some time and unbeknown to my mum, he was sucked into the world of race gambling.

The atmosphere at home changed. I heard Dave raise his voice at Mum and slam doors from my bedroom upstairs. I didn't like it. It scared me. I started to feel anxious, on the edge of high alert for the next blow-up to happen. I had no idea why Dave kept shouting and slamming doors and smashing things. It wasn't open for discussion. Mum kept the peace and life muddled on.

THE AGE OF COMPARISON

SEPTEMBER 1985

I'm standing in Mum's ensuite bathroom. I've just got out of the bath; my hair is still dripping. There is a large mirror hung above the sink and one balanced on the windowsill. Two mirrors, two angles.

I'm staring at myself.

You've such a fat face.

Your breasts are small but your nipples are huge, urgh.

You're so short. Why can't you be taller?

I touch my round belly. I don't look like the women in magazines. Or the girls at school, who are tall and thin.

Urgh, fat belly.

I can pinch too much skin around my middle.

Where's my waist? The one I'm meant to have?

Mum has a set of weighing scales in here. *I wonder how much I weigh? I'm going to check.*

I hop on the white scales and the black needle quivers before settling on a number.

If I stop eating so much maybe I could lose weight? If I'm thinner, then maybe I will look taller too? If I'm thinner, then my friends will really like me and maybe I will be happy?

I know what I am going to do. I'm going to start a diet tomorrow.

Within a year of the wedding, Dave's son moved in with us, then Dave's elderly mother when her health started to fail. For a time, there were six of us living together in a blended family.

To make ends meet, Mum often took in young students who had come to England to learn the language. She juggled her job as a bookkeeper, as well as running the house and caring for her new elderly mother-in-law. Mum was a hard labourer both physically and emotionally and waited on every one hand and foot. I never saw her complain though. She was too tired and had accepted her new way of life. My dad finally accepted it too and decided to leave for good. This time for the distant shores of Western Australia.

I settled into my secondary school and befriended two girls during my first year: Sarah and Kerry. Sarah was an only child, tall and athletic with skin that tanned easily. She lived in a beautiful four-bedroom home in an even more beautiful tree-lined suburb with fabulous parents and her two pet cats. Sarah was everything I wasn't: tall and slim, confident and sharp-witted. I envied her, both her body shape and popularity.

Kerry was slim, arty and very individual in her style. She was just *so* cool. Her home was an unusually quirky cottage, tastefully decorated in Laura Ashley wallpaper and soft furnishings. Her parents seemed cool too and like Sarah's, they were still married. I admired both girls and their normal families.

I, on the other hand, was much shorter, well-rounded with pale skin that only ever burnt or freckled and a mop of overly frizzy chestnut-brown curls. Things at home had become unpredictable and sometimes volatile with Dave and his unexpected angry outbursts. I rarely invited anyone home to my house. It felt too chaotic and I wanted to make it easier for Mum.

I *hated* school sports and seemed to have two left feet when it came to any attempt at exercise. I was a clumsy competitor and sports lessons filled me with dread. Our sports kit consisted of navy shorts, cut like unforgivingly short hot pants and a white polo top, regardless of the weather. So even during the depths of winter, we were forced to run through frost-covered fields. The cold stung our bare legs and turned our knees blue.

Ms Duggan, our PE teacher, would chase behind us with seemingly unending energy and a shrill whistle to round up the stragglers, one of whom was always me. "Come along, girls, hurry up!" she'd bark with the bellowing voice of a drill sergeant that didn't match her 4' 11" frame. Those scantily clad sports sessions in all weathers were encouraged as character-building for us and were followed by the threat of a lukewarm communal shower if we made it back in time.

Please don't make us shower together. I hate how my body looks, I'd think.

I was a shy girl by nature and as I moved into my teenage years, my embarrassment about my new body shape grew along with it. Swimming lessons were the worst. Stripping off to get changed into my sports kit in front of the other girls was bad enough. I didn't want *anyone* to see my breasts, even if they were covered in a bra, or my big hips and bare legs, or my bum in navy pants. But to strip off completely to change into a bathing suit was the *pièce de résistance* of my body-shape distress: naked flesh, pubic hair, blue pimply skin from the cold with frozen, hard nipples. I'd cover my bits as best I could with my hands spread out, knees bent in, touching for added 'privates' privacy and prayed for it to all be over quickly. I'd race to get changed back into my uniform as quickly as possible whilst everyone else was distracted with dressing and chatting. It meant there was less chance of anyone seeing my body.

Sometimes I'd sit on the wooden bench in the changing rooms waiting for the others as they gossiped. I was curious about the other girls' bodies. Some looked so different to mine, like Sarah's, or Jessica's, or Kimberly's and Ann-Marie's: taller, thinner, bigger breasts. That's how bodies were meant to look, I thought. That's what made them beautiful, right? Why couldn't I look like them too? *You're just short and fat, Emily*, my troll reminded me.

It began as a harmless diet to slim my blossoming body. I wanted to be like the other girls at school, the tall, thin popular ones. I wanted to look like the popstars in music videos too and the models in magazines: tall and thin, confident and beautiful.

It was a gradual thing to begin with. First, I stopped eating chocolate, cakes, biscuits and crisps; no more of Mum's wee buns. These were *bad* foods. I knew that. Mum's weekly magazines confirmed it and so did the diet adverts on television. Low-fat foods were eaten by thin women. Exercise videos featured women in skin-tight pink leotards. Pinching loose skin was a bad thing. I'd seen it all and it had sunk in.

I would skip breakfast most days. Then I started to leave food in my lunch box, half-eaten. I'd allow myself a bite or two of my sandwiches but that was all. Everything else was left untouched. My school uniform began to feel looser on me and that pleased me.

Better ... but you're still fat though, Emily, my troll would say.

Mum didn't question it to begin with and when she started to, I just threw the rest of the sandwich away in the school bin and gave the other bits away in the playground to whoever would take them. It stopped Mum asking questions. Sometimes I would pour a little cereal in a bowl and pour over some milk, enough to make it soggy, before tipping it all down the sink. I'd run the tap to get rid of it but leave enough in the bowl to make it look like I'd eaten something. I'd put a knife in the peanut-butter jar and smear some on then wipe it off, before putting the knife on a plate in the sink. I learned to be sneaky; magic tricks with food.

I began weighing myself secretly in Mum's bathroom every now and again. The black needle kept settling on a smaller number each time and that pleased me too. I scrutinised my reflection in her mirror after every bath, searching for evidence that I was losing weight. *Keep it up, Emily, you're getting slimmer*, I'd tell myself.

Mum cooked dinner every night and we all used to sit down together to eat. Under different circumstances, family dinner-time together should have made a welcome change. But after a while, it became a nightly event filled with anxiety. I would pick at my dinner and push the rest of my food around the plate, disguising lumps of meat under vegetables. I became quite the plate artist, adept at food camouflage, making it appear as if I'd consumed far more than I had. The thought of eating it began to repulse me. Not because of the taste – I was so hungry, I *wanted* to eat – but because of the thought of all the calories it would mean ingesting.

"Urgh, Ryan, you are so disgusting. Stop eating like a pig!"

"Shut up, Emily," Ryan barked back.

"That's enough you two. Eat your dinner, not another word!" Mum snapped.

I'd observe Ryan as he'd hungrily devour his dinner with a teenage boy's enthusiastic appetite and it revolted me.

Since childhood, Mum had always dished up generous portions of food. As the need to diet intensified, I had to lessen my food intake without anyone noticing. The only bonus of

Ryan's revolting table habits was that he always willingly took my surplus food.

"Ryan, do you want these roast potatoes too? Mum's given me too many." I'd stab the potatoes and hover over Ryan's plate, ready to offload them. Then I'd slide a slice of roast beef over, maybe a Yorkshire pudding too. He hadn't worked out what I was doing, he was too busy tucking into Mum's piles of food.

I had to remain discreet in my behaviour, so I'd watch Mum, Ryan and Dave's eating style and clatter my cutlery on my plate with appropriate bursts to sync with everyone else's rhythm. I would 'accidentally' drop chunks of food on the floor so that Sam, our dog who sat under the dining table, could eagerly hoover it up in seconds, sparing me from having to. Nobody noticed. Sam was my secret ally.

The benefit of a large, blended family and a household of students was that it was always noisy and chaotic around dinnertime so no one noticed my quiet avoidance for a long time. *Good girl Emily, you barely ate a thing*, the troll said.

As things escalated at home with Dave's often explosive behaviour, I felt bewildered and invisible. My mum had her hands full. Dad was gone and incommunicado. The changes in my eating habits became less of a diet and developed into something much darker. I got a kick out of the hunger pangs, a sense of control from denying myself food. My troll became more active, telling me, *You are still too fat; you need to eat less.*

With every meal that I skipped, with every hungry sensation I experienced, I felt more powerful. I believed I had incredible willpower to ignore the gnawing hunger pains and saw it as strength. The weigh-ins became daily and ritualised. My troll became louder.

I tried every trick in the book to avoid the dinner table as this was the only meal that bore witness to my behaviour and my family had started to notice my dinnertime games. I'd make excuses to my Mum about the endless amounts of homework I had to do and would take my dinner to my room to eat whilst working. Only I didn't eat much at all, tipping it all in my bedroom bin. I'd wrap up the bag and hide it under my bed until Mum was at work the next day, then I'd bury it in my school bag under my books and throw it outside in the rubbish bin. If Dave was about, I'd dump it in a bin on the way to school.

"Jesus, Mary and Joseph, Emily, you're wasting away!" Mum cried, as she wrapped her arms around me.

"Get off me, Mum, leave me alone." I pulled away from her grip. "Stop making a fuss."

Please make a fuss of me, Mum. I feel so alone.

"Emily, love, you need to eat more, you're getting far too thin," Mum reminded me.

"No, I don't! Look at my face, it's so fat, look at my stomach!"

"Ah Jesus, Emily, no you don't..." Mum sighed and walked away, back to Dave and a different problem.

STARVING

JULY 1986

I'M STANDING IN MUM'S BEDROOM IN FRONT OF THE FULL-length mirror. I've just got out of the bath in her ensuite. Mum's busy downstairs in the kitchen making dinner. I can smell it cooking, a roast dinner, I think.

I'm *so* hungry, my mouth is watering. I want to eat something but I'm not allowed to.

No, Emily, don't be weak.

I'm dripping wet and shivering. I feel cold to core of my body all the time. I like my baths though. My body disappears under the bubbles. I feel weightless. That's where I want to be. Weightless and hidden. I like my baths really hot; they warm me up after school and I can sit alone for ages, just me and my thoughts.

If I have a really hot bath, maybe it will burn more calories?

I must shave my legs and my arms. If every hair is gone, I will weigh less.

I must wash all this conditioner out properly; it might weigh something.

I must rub all the dry skin off my body; I will weigh less.

Wait, what if this bath water goes in through my skin? I wonder if it weighs something?

I don't want to look in the mirror but at the same time, I do. I'm torn. I want to see my progress, I want to see if this diet is working, but I'm scared too.

What if it's not enough? What if I'm not thin enough?

I stare at her, the naked, wet girl in the mirror.

Who is she? I don't know her. She is so fat and ugly.

I can't see her really, not clearly. I can't see her shrinking body. Her bones poking out where flesh should be. She has painfully thin arms and sparrow's legs. She has no bum left really. She has no belly.

It's not enough, Emily.

I hate myself.

"Oi fatty, eat a cheeseburger!" A boy laughed at me and his mates joined in. My face flushed red and my heart began pumping.

I looked over without moving my head, just my eyes. I needed to see who had noticed how fat I was, still. I didn't recognise him or his sarcasm, although I'd heard every word, all I heard was "fatty".

A group of schoolboys were standing around smoking on the other side of the road, just past my school railings, their school bags thrown in an unruly heap on the pavement. The cool boys from the local boy's school were waiting for the cool girls to arrive at my school. They often did: the boys started later than us so they'd steal a few minutes to mingle and smoke together before school began.

No one ever noticed me. But that morning someone did and he called me fatty. He had only noticed me because I was fat and my weight had made him and his mates laugh at me. The lump in my throat felt like a boulder, threatening to choke me.

Please don't cry. Please don't cry, I tell myself.

I hurried past them as they laughed and sneered at me, Fat Emily.

The diet clearly wasn't working. It was time to be more disciplined.

As the weeks passed, I became even more obsessed with food and my body weight and it led me to damaging restriction. It's not that I didn't feel hungry, I did a lot of the time and when the hunger growled painfully in my belly, I'd begin to feel anxious because it signalled the time to be strong and resist once again. I never lost my appetite, I just learnt to control it. There was a strange sense of euphoria each time I had successfully denied it.

I'd often switch between repulsion and longing over food. I could salivate looking at Mum's dinners but convince myself they were bad for me, that they would make me fatter than I already was. It didn't stop the natural physical instinct of my body to need food, but my troll overrode it, with disturbing success.

I restricted food almost exclusively to half a raw carrot and a few bites of a green apple a day, plus sips of water, nothing more. I discovered a new trick: a drink of water took away the hunger pains, but only for a while.

As soon as I woke up in the morning, I'd reach for my belly. I needed to feel if the apple I'd nibbled on the night before had made me gain weight. Was it my imagination or was I more bloated?

I'd feel my arms, my legs and cheeks. I'd wrap my fingers around my wrists, measuring them. I wanted them to shrink. I'd pinch my skin and any excess confirmed to me I still had a long way to go to reach my goal: thinner and therefore beautiful.

I began to refuse Mum's lifts home after school; I needed the exercise to enhance the calorie deficit. At school I'd quietly rock my feet, heel to toe under my desk, or shake my leg rapidly. I was constantly in motion because those movements counted, no matter how small and discreet, and they would help counteract the calories I'd consume from that day's carrots and apples.

It was an obsession, an overwhelming, life-altering one. I thought about food constantly, every waking minute spent thinking about every aspect of food: its content, its calorific value, its smell, its texture and taste. The obsession fuelled my focus on my body shape and everything in my environment that could potentially alter my weight, real or imagined.

I thought I was being smart, that no one had noticed, but of course, I was wrong. The weight had been falling off me and Mum had been watching her daughter shrink in front of her eyes. She saw the bones slowly appearing that should have been covered in pubescent flesh, the protruding hips, the ribs and collar bone. When she would lean in to embrace me, her shock was palpable and she would start to cry. And yet I still couldn't understand why she would get so upset.

"Ah Jesus, Emily, you'll end up like that singer, dead and buried. You *need* to eat!"

It was easy to disguise my weight loss at the time. I hid in baggy jeans and oversized T-shirts that were fashionable in the mid-eighties. Layers of clothes under a thick winter coat covered my disappearing frame, but clothes couldn't disguise my pale skin, sunken eyes or fatigue – nor did they stop me feeling constantly cold.

After months of restriction and getting worryingly thin, Mum insisted on taking me to the doctor – she gave me no choice in the matter. In 1985, there was no talk of eating disorders at school or specialised treatment – the local doctor's surgery was the only place Mum knew to go.

"Come in, come in," the doctor said dismissively.

Mum led the way. I followed her in, unwillingly.

A man in his late fifties sat at his desk, pulls his metal-rimmed reading glasses down to the edge of his nose to get a better look at me. "What can I do for you today?" he enquired, glancing from Mum to me.

It was late afternoon and getting dark outside. He must have seen many patients before us, he sounded irritated.

"Well, it's my daughter, Emily, here. She's not eating you see, doctor, and she's lost so much weight. I'm so worried about..." Mum trailed off. She was already crying.

Please don't cry, Mum, I thought.

"I see ... and how long has this been going on?" His gaze turned to me. I looked at the floor and shuffled my feet.

I didn't want to talk about this.

"Well, a good few months now, doctor."

"Right then, young lady, take your skirt and jumper off and get up on here," he ordered as he pulled a faded blue curtain across the front of the couch.

I looked at Mum stricken with fear. *Please don't make me strip off here, not in front of him,* I plead silently. My expression said it all, I didn't need to speak.

"Come on, Emily, love. Do what the doctor says now," Mum encouraged. Her tears said it all. She didn't need to speak either.

I slipped behind the curtain and stripped down to my pants and bra, unbuttoning my school-uniform shirt, folding it across me. I couldn't bear to remove it. I laid on the bed and my hip bones jutted upwards. I could see them. My belly was less than flat. Sloping inward. Non-existent. Here was my evidence that this diet was paying off.

"Right, young lady. Let's take a look at you."

The doctor pulled the curtain back. Mum was sitting in the corner silently crying.

Suddenly I feel tiny and helpless, like a fragile bird, undressed and exposed under the bright white lights in this sterile room with a strange man and his cold hands. He pulls my shirt open without a thought for my discomfort and leans down with a cold metal stethoscope to listen to my heart. He's so close I can see the hairs in his nose. I can smell coffee on his stale breath. I swear my heart is beating faster because of him.

"Hmm..." he mutters to himself.

He pokes and prods around my body, my shoulder blades, my ribs, my spine – examining me. He rests his palms on my belly for a moment and then pushes them down. The pressure hurts. He feels my jutting hips, my pelvis and the rest of my slowly shrinking frame.

"Are you still menstruating?" he asks matter-of-factly.

This is so embarrassing.

"No ... not really," I whisper.

"You're at risk of damaging your reproductive system if you continue with this starving business. Do you want to have children? If you carry on like this, you won't be able to."

I'm fourteen. I don't care about having kids, I've never even given it a thought. I just want to be slim. Slimmer will make me happier.

The doctor turns to look at Mum briefly, then back to me. "Look at your mother over there crying. Look at what you are doing to her!" he scolds. "Right, young lady, hop down and get dressed. I'm going to weigh you."

Oh no, please don't weigh me here, not in front of you, not in front of Mum. Not fully clothed. That won't be real.

I dress behind the curtain and reappear. I stand on the big metal scales and the black needle quivers and settles.

"Six stone, five pounds and two ounces," he reads out and turns to my notes to record my numbers.

Here's my reward for this dieting.

Mum put her hands to her mouth to stifle her gasp and catch her tears.

The doctor turns to Mum and lowers his glasses to the edge of his nose once more. "I believe your daughter has anorexia nervosa, an eating disorder. She needs to start eating properly."

Then he turns to me. "This is very serious, Emily. I want to see you again in one week and if you haven't gained weight in that time period, I'm going to admit you to hospital and they will feed you through a tube in your nose. Is that what you want? To be force-fed?" he asks firmly.

"No..." I shake my head, fearfully.

"Right then, young lady – one week." He stands to signal for us to leave. It feels like I'm in trouble in school and this is detention.

"Please ensure she starts to eat," he warns Mum in the same tone.

Maybe she is in trouble too? It's all my fault.

"Jesus, Mary and Joseph, Emily, six stone five!" Mum cries, grabbing my arm as we walk towards the car. "Oh Emily, love, you worry me to death. Sure, there's nothing of you. Did you hear what your man said to you? You *have* to start eating," she pleads.

I'm so sorry, Mum, I never meant to worry you.

"Yes, Mum, I heard..." I say sheepishly, head down, scuffling my feet.

Yes, I heard him. Every word.

We were sent away with nothing. No help, just a threat to hospitalise me if I didn't start eating. Mum was left to pull me back from the grasp of a full-blown eating disorder alone. I had no idea how close I was to being hospitalised, or worse, if I didn't start eating.

So, this 'thing' I was doing, this diet was actually an illness and it had a name: anorexia nervosa. I had heard the term mentioned before on TV. The American singer Karen Carpenter had died from health complications caused by anorexia a couple of years earlier and another British TV star, Lena Zavaroni, was suffering with it. I had heard Mum talk about them both, but it never occurred to me I had it too. I didn't know I was sick. Back then, there was no internet or search engines. No Dr Google to self-diagnose. That was probably not a bad thing.

I was terrified at the prospect of being hospitalised and force-fed and I reluctantly vowed to try eating just a little bit more from then on, mostly for my mum's sake, but it wasn't easy. In fact, it felt like torture. On some level, I almost felt grateful that something belonged just to me, even if it was a mental-health disorder.

A couple of days after the doctor's visit, I remember getting out of the shower and seeing myself in the full-length mirror. Dave had fitted it in the downstairs bathroom along with several spotlights – the kind of bright white lights that gave an unforgivingly harsh reality check on everything. I rarely used the downstairs bathroom, mostly because of that lighting, but that day, one of the students had been monopolising the upstairs bathroom doing her hair for what felt like an age.

As I stepped onto the mat, wrapping the towel around my thin frame, I caught something from the corner of my mascara-blackened eyes and it prompted me to look properly. I let the towel fall away and settle on my feet, my shroud of safety voluntarily surrendered. It was incredibly uncomfortable, yet a macabre curiosity drove me to stare at my body, dripping and uncovered. Perhaps the doctor's jarring words, still fresh in my mind, were more impactful than I had realised at the time. Finally, I could see myself for the first time the way my mum saw me. I looked skeletal. How had I not seen myself that way before? I didn't understand it.

Dear Mrs Orchard

I am writing to tell you my daughter, Emily, has been diagnosed with anorexia and is under doctor's orders to eat. She can't do any sports for now. I'm going to be changing my hours at work soon so I can watch her at home more, but for now I'd be grateful if you tell all her teachers and keep a close eye on her. It's a real worry for me.

Thank you
Yours faithfully
Catherine Johnson

That morning, Mum insisted on driving me to school and delivering her hand-written letter to the school office personally. Now all eyes were on me and my recovery. I was excused from school sports and got to sit in the library alone, reading.

I had overly concerned teachers watching my every move at

school, keeping an eye on me at lunchtimes and paying a little extra attention to me during lessons. They did it discreetly, but not so discreet that I didn't notice.

Mum cut her hours in the office and did bookwork from home, to ensure I was eating something.

BELLY

1986

"Emily, love, come and sit with me."

I sit down at the table. It's Saturday lunchtime and the house is unusually quiet. It's just me and Mum.

A plate is in front of me. On it lies half a peanut-butter sandwich cut into bitesize pieces.

Am I toddler again?

"Mum, I'm fourteen! You don't need to cut up my food."

"Emily, have a wee bite. Please, love."

I look at all the pieces. I count them. All six of them. This is a mound of food I can't possibly eat.

I pick up one piece and put it to my lips. I can hear Mum, she's stopped breathing. She's waiting.

I put it in. My throat closes, I don't want to eat this. It's so salty and soft and full of peanut pieces. And fat and calories.

The flavour is so strong. I push it past my tongue and swallow hard. Please get this over and done with. I want to please her.

"Well done, love, have another one. Now, tell me the *craic* at school today. What went on?"

It's hard to describe in words how it would make me feel trying to eat in those early days of recovery; the mental battles I'd go through putting food in my mouth followed by the overwhelming feeling of needing to compensate for the calorie intake somehow. It took a long time to unpick those thoughts and in all honesty, I never did.

Mum sat with me every single evening with a small plate of food, a dinner the size of a young child's: two potatoes, one thin slice of beef and a mouthful of vegetables with a drizzle of gravy. Not that much by anyone else's standards, but it still felt like a huge portion to me.

Mum was very careful, especially in the early weeks, not to overwhelm me. We would talk about my day at school. Sometimes it could take well over an hour for me to start to pick at the food, but Mum sat there patiently, night after night. She didn't pressure me, or scold me, she distracted me and I slowly began to eat.

I gradually regained some weight. Sometimes I stayed the same for a week or two and maintained my weight rather than gained anything, but Mum never criticised me, she carried on feeding me slowly.

For a long time, my shape and weight was the *only* thing I had focused on and I despised the weight gain. At the same time, I had accepted I had an eating disorder and that regaining weight was part of my recovery. Knowing that, it still didn't take away my discomfort with it. For so long, food had been my nemesis and I battled to put every morsel in my mouth. Without professional therapy to address the cause, or any form of medical treatment, it was my battle alone and the only way I knew how to recover was to slowly start eating.

I remember going on a school skiing trip to France a few months into my recovery. I had pleaded with my mum to go, desperate to keep up with Sarah and Kerry who were both going. I just wanted to be like everyone else. I begged Mum for the £150 or so, but that was a lot of money for someone who was already working and looking after the overseas students to make ends meet (and keep up with my gambling stepfather's habits). Finally, she gave in and found the money somehow. She said the break in routine would do me good. *Maybe the break from me would do her good too,* I reasoned.

It was on that school trip that I noticed my Home Economics teacher paying particular attention to me during mealtimes. As I sat amongst my group of friends, lined up at long trestle tables for meals, she would hover nearby to ensure I was eating something. I was still picking at food at that stage – it had only been six months since my telling off at the doctor's. But at least I was eating small amounts again; I just wished I didn't have a concerned audience watching me every time.

Our group was mixed with boys from another travelling school. It was a heady mix of raging teenage hormones, especially for a group of pubescent girls from an all-girls school. Despite my shyness, I fell for one lad, my first-ever crush.

"Hey, Belly!" Dean grins at me. "How did you get on the slopes today?"

I blush. "Um ... okay."

I didn't really, I nearly broke my neck on the ice.

Oh no, he's noticed my belly! Does he see it's flat? Wait, maybe he thinks it's fat?!

"I have to go. See you later..."

"See ya, Belly," Dean grins.

I leave Dean standing and make a beeline for the cloakroom with the mirror. I need to see what he saw.

Is my belly sticking out again?

I turn to the side but I don't see a belly, its concave. The one I used to have is now sunken in. I run my hand over the inward dip. It satisfies me.

So that's why he noticed my belly, it's because it's not there!

He likes me because I am thin.

Dean was a favourite amongst the girls, me included, though I never thought he would notice me, but he did. He said I was cute and he'd given me a nickname: Belly.

Dean was confident and cheeky with a crown of thick blond hair and beautiful blue eyes that almost disappeared when he smiled; a smile that lit up the dining hall we sat in every day. At fourteen years old, he was already full of charm,and it worked on the girls like magic, me included. I remember him smiling at me, singling me out for a chat in the recreation room. Dean was the first boy I'd really spoken to since primary school. Segregated schools didn't exactly prepare you for mingling with the opposite sex.

Before breakfast the next morning, I pulled in the belt on my yellow all-in-one ski suit as tight as I could, until it pinched and hurt. It padded my body out and made me look bigger than the body beneath it and I was determined to do something about it.

There, that's better. Now I have no belly AND they can see my waist, I thought.

At the time, I was still very underweight. Belly was a harmless nickname to Dean. He thought it was a bit of a joke, a funny compliment in front of new friends, but it reinforced my belief that thin was beautiful. I liked the attention Dean paid me and convinced myself it was because I was thin. It wasn't difficult – my anorexic mind was still very active.

I was fourteen years old and in the fourth year of secondary school. Being a July baby left me one of the youngest in my year group. Over the previous twelve months, I had slowly drifted from my friendship with Sarah and Kerry as they climbed the academic ranks into different sets above me and I found myself in a new all-girl friendship triangle with Joanne and Katie who lived nearby me. Katie was a little taller than me, with permed brown curls, huge eyes and voluptuous breasts to match. She knew exactly what she was doing with clothes and make-up. She had an eye for fashion and her legs looked incredible in her pastel-pink puffball skirt and crop-top ensemble.

Katie heavily outlined her eyes with black kohl and layer upon layer of black mascara every day for school, despite the teachers' objections and being given a tissue to wipe it off in the school toilets. She'd complete the look with an iridescent pink lipstick that made her lips appear almost white. So very eighties. So very cool.

Joanne was stunning. Model-tall, thin frame with golden-tanned legs up to her armpits and long, honey-blonde hair. She looked like the women in magazines. Joanne could have worn a sack and made it look great. Boys loved her, girls envied her. She was beautiful. Both girls modelled occasionally for a local clothes boutique at amateur fashion shows.

I *so* wanted to be like them. They both lived at home with

their still-married parents. Katie's parents were warm and nurturing and clearly deeply in love. Katie's dad, Martin, doted on her.

"Love you, my angel!" Martin would always greet his daughter with a kiss on her cheek as Katie smiled and quietly cringed. I often stayed over there. It was a home filled with love.

I remained very underweight and living in a self-created shadow of my two model friends. I felt like the runt of the friendship litter. It wasn't true at all, but I'd demoted myself there. Katie and Joanne were lovely girls and great friends to me but I always wondered what I offered to them. I was very shy and rarely wore make-up or experimented with clothes. It was easier to hide my frame in the same baggy clothes and divert attention from my body in recovery.

I still hadn't reconciled myself with the new, slightly bigger body I was in. I was obsessed with my belly. I wanted it to remain concave, but it didn't. As I gradually regained weight all over my body, it naturally began to fill out. It was no longer sunken in, just flat. I missed my concave belly. I mourned my anorexic shape.

Whilst my friends often hung out at the local burger bar in town, I found excuses to avoid joining them. I didn't want to sit in the restaurant explaining why I didn't want to eat burgers and fries. There was no fun in it for me. I still wasn't that comfortable eating in front of people and I didn't want all eyes on me with every meal. My schoolfriends knew I was recovering from anorexia and they thought that encouraging me to eat with them was helpful to me. But all I could think about was how many fries covered in oil were in a serving and how many calories they contained. It was just easier to make up an excuse not to go but that discomfort and avoidance was leading me to isolation.

I'd grown tired of the long, brown, frizzy curls I'd always had and needed something to change how I felt about myself. I felt like the boring ugly duckling with two model swan friends. I'd had the same un-styled hair since I was a child and although thick and curly, it lacked any shape. I decided on a DIY haircut one afternoon after school when Mum was still at work. I hacked at my hair with her dressmaking scissors until it was longer on one side. As my natural curls were cut, they shrank considerably and I ended up with an unintentional bob and a side fringe that resembled a small woolly sheep, which did nothing for my fragile confidence.

When Mum returned from work, she was less than impressed with my self-styled make over. *"Jesus, Mary and Joseph, Emily, what have you done?! You've scalped yourself!"* she groaned, tutting as she ran her fingers through my scraggy cut. Mum had always told me my hair was my crowning glory and in one short afternoon I'd butchered it.

Mum did her best to repair the damage and chopped it even shorter, evening out the shape at least, but now my curls sprung up even more and were sitting just below my ears.

I cried my eyes out, devastated with the short style. I couldn't disguise it – it wasn't even long enough to properly tie up. It's strange how a hairstyle can make you feel so different: a great cut and restyle could put me on top of the world, but a bad chop made me feel like my world was over, at least it did at fourteen years old. My one saving grace was that my hair grew reasonably quickly so within a few months, I could pull it in to the smallest of hairbands at my neck and back comb the fringe into an acceptably big eighties style.

That autumn, Katie, Joanne and I started to hang out in the evenings on a local street corner. It was the intersection of three roads – one, a busy main road – with three wooden benches that sat outside the local churchyard wall.

Being near two bus stops and a late-night shop, it was the perfect pit-stop for the local youth. It had no shelter and that winter, the bitter wind howled across the open crossroads, but in the absence of a youth club or anywhere better to hang out, the benches were the next best thing.

Joanne and Katie both had boyfriends – all the girls that hung out there did – and they would sit across the boys' laps, legs wrapped around them, kissing and smoking whilst I stood on the side, shuffling awkwardly.

On the chilly winter nights, they'd all share bags of steaming-hot chips from the local chippy whilst I watched on, standing under its tired plastic canopy for some welcome shelter from the rain. I still couldn't eat chips – they were forbidden to me. Sometimes the eldest lad of the group would take a chance and try to buy cider for the group from the local shop.

Someone had drawn a picture of a fridge in the local park shelter and scrawled '*Em J*' underneath. I found out sometime later that it was a group of lads from the nearby boys' school. I was just fifteen and had never been kissed; because I was shy and hadn't put out, the local lads assumed I was also frigid.

One of the lads at the benches was John. He was seventeen and looked like a young Tom Cruise with his thick, jet-black hair. John was shy like me and lived in the road behind mine, so we would often walk home together for my 9pm curfew. John always looked out for me and I liked that. He made me feel safe and less alone. He didn't seem to mind my shy quirkiness and baggy clothes, or that I was pale and obviously still very underweight.

That New Year's Eve, John was in the town centre bringing in the new year with his mates and a fake ID. Katie, Joanne and I had gone into town to wander around. They were meeting their boyfriends and I was playing third wheel. We had no chance of getting into pubs at our age but just to be in the town centre surrounded by revellers at midnight felt exciting.

I bumped into John just after midnight and with the courage of four brown ales, he wished me a happy new year and kissed me – my first kiss.

Two weeks later, I had my first boyfriend. I was fifteen, John was seventeen.

MONTELUPONE

JUNE 1988

Above the heavy wooden table, a fan whirs lazily, creating little change or cool breeze in the room. The dining room is dim. It's lunchtime, but the shutters are almost fully closed to deny the heat of the day from entering. Bright sunshine bathes green vines and bursts of pink blooms through the wooden slats. A television balanced on an old wooden dressing unit is playing garishly loud adverts in Italian. I'm grateful for the noisy interruption to break the awkwardness I'm feeling.

Giuseppe, a man well into his seventies, is sitting at the end of the table in a white vest and beige trousers, staring at me silently with a mixture of curiosity and caution. His hairy arms are on display and dense grey hair pokes out around the top off his vest.

His son, Alessandro, takes his seat at the table next to his father and shortly after, Giovanna joins us. She looks at me warily, clearly not that keen on sharing her family home with a strange English girl. The table has an unlabelled bottle of home-made wine and a bottle of aqua frizzante on it.

"Emily, you like water, how you say it ... bubbles?" Sofia quizzes.

"Oh, you mean fizzy. No, no – tap water is fine, thank you," I reply.

The rest of the family look at Sofia for a translation. Giovanna looks at me and mutters something unimpressed. I've never tried fizzy water and I'm not about to try now with an audience.

Alessandro leans back on his chair, turning his head towards the large wooden doors at the end of the dining room and calls to his wife, Rosa, who is busy in the kitchen. *"Rosa, portami ancora acqua per la ragazza,"* he bellows.

Rosa appears moments later with a bottle of iced still water for me and a sweat on her brow, clearly flustered at having been interrupted from her business in the hot kitchen. She places it before me and disappears back into the kitchen.

Giulia, a tiny woman in height and stature, opens the door for Rosa who proudly carries a huge dish of pasta and sets it down in front of me. Rosa has a kind face but the expression and energy of a woman who works far too hard for her family. She bends down and puts her arm around me and whispers something in Italian, as she squeezes my shoulders together.

Sofia laughs. "*Troppo magro* – she says you are too thin and need to eat."

Sofia's family all laugh together – it seems they are in agreement. This family are all a healthy weight and I'm just over a year into my recovery from anorexia. Suddenly I am the centre of eating attention again.

They think you're strange, Emily.

Rosa takes a plate for me and piles a mound of glistening oily pasta onto it. I put my hand up to stop her, the serving is already far more than I can eat. It looks plain – it's neither dripping in Bolognese sauce or cheese – the way Mum serves it at home. Only a little olive oil, basil leaves and fresh tomato sauce dress the pasta.

They are all watching me silently, I know it. I daren't look at them but I feel their stare. I stab a piece with my fork and put it in my mouth. Its delicate flavours and freshness melt on my tongue. "Mmm, it's delicious, thank you!"

I smile at Rosa who appears to be holding her breath, waiting for my approval. She glances at Sophia for confirmation.

"*Ha detto che e deliziosa, mamma,*" Sophia confirms for her mother. Rosa visibly relaxes and smiles at me approvingly.

"*Molto bene.*" She smiles, putting her hands on my shoulders from behind and squeezing them tightly. Rosa is clearly proud of her cooking, but perhaps she also feels obliged to make it her mission to feed me up.

Oh no, did Mum tell her about my anorexia?

The family had been all closely watching me, waiting for my response. Maybe they all know?

I place my fork down on the plate, glistening from the oily pasta residue. I feel such a sense of accomplishment having finished all the pasta on my plate. The light, fresh flavour is beautiful but I'm silently counting the calories I have consumed. I *never* eat plates of pasta.

Within minutes, Rosa arrives with another dish filled with golden chicken pieces and a tray of potatoes roasted with garlic and rosemary twigs. My heart sinks. I want to get on the first plane home now to my mum and the safety of my bedroom in rainy England. But I can't. This is my idea of hell.

I help myself to a small piece of chicken and some strips of roasted potato out of politeness as my audience are observing me. Rosa is standing beside me, gesturing to add more as she reaches for the serving utensils.

'Oh no, thank you, that is enough, honestly." I pat my belly and try to block her from piling any more on my plate. Some hand gestures are universally understood.

I'm already full and way out of my comfort zone with food and another six pairs of eyes are watching my every mouthful. Rosa mutters something and I can feel her disproval at my small appetite.

"*Mamma lasciala stara, basta*!' Sofia exclaims.

'I'm telling her that is enough for you," she reassures me, aware of my obvious discomfort.

"*Tut!*" Rosa rolls her eyes, with motherly frustration more than anything else.

And with that, Rosa takes her seat at the table and they all begin eating. Suddenly it is a noisy dining room filled with clattering cutlery and passionate loud conversation amongst a close-knit family with wonderful homecooked food.

I left school after my exams were complete at the end of May 1988. Mum had received a letter from one the families of the young students, Sofia, a sixteen-year-old Italian girl she had cared for earlier in the year. They wanted to extend an invitation to me to spend the summer with them in their village in Italy to help their daughter improve her English.

I think Mum secretly wanted me to go because I'd been dating John for five months and her concerns for me sinning and ending up pregnant were growing. Unbeknown to her, I was still very much a virgin and I had no intention of losing that badge any time soon. But mostly, she thought the change of scene would help and being around all that pasta would help me re-gain weight. And so, aged fifteen, I was put on a plane alone and sent to Ancona in Eastern Italy.

As the plane landed at the small airport and taxied to a halt,

I was glued to the window. Everything seemed parched dry and bathed in warm golden light. It was so different to the familiar green grass and grey skies of England that I'd left behind.

Sofia and her father were waiting for me at the airport and although I didn't know Sofia all that well, her face was welcomingly familiar in a foreign land. She extended her arms and lightly kissed me on each cheek, her lips barely touching my skin. I wasn't used to such a personal greeting and I blushed at her touch.

"Welcome, Emily, welcome. *Mio padre*, Alessandro... my father, I mean." Sofia laughed shyly as she led me to her father who was standing smiling at me, looking as awkward with the exchange as I was feeling.

"*Ciao, ciao*. Hello." He smiled and gently kissed my cheeks. I felt a touch of his unshaven chin and caught a fleeting smell of cologne.

"Hello!" I smiled back, blushing from his kisses, unable to muster the courage to say *ciao*.

Alessandro took my case and put it in the car and Sofia and I climbed in. The journey was painfully silent to begin with and I wondered why I had agreed to travel to Italy alone, to stay with people I didn't know, who spoke a language I didn't understand.

I arrived with no understanding of Italian culture, just the knowledge that spaghetti came from there and that they had a leaning tower named after pizza. I didn't have the sense before I left to head to the local library to read more about the place I'd be spending my summer in.

Sofia became translator as her father asked simple questions of me, glancing from time to time in his rear-view mirror and catching my eyes as he smiled warmly.

Alessandro drove along the motorway for an hour or so and as we neared his hometown, he must have seen my gaze shift from him to the passing fields filled with green crops that swayed in fluid waves in the afternoon breeze. "*Ecco qui.* Montelupone," Alessandro declared proudly.

I turned to Sofia for confirmation. Was this my new summer home?

Sofia smiled. "Here it is – this is my home."

There before us sat a village at the top of a hill. A collection of stone sugar cube-shaped buildings, surrounded by high brown-stone walls. Even the name rolled off their tongues and its beautiful surroundings matched. It was the most picturesque place I had ever seen, a step back into a forgotten time, with medieval brick buildings, wooden shutters on windows, terracotta pots of brightly coloured geraniums and lazy cats curled up on steps, basking in the hot June sunshine. This was to be my home for the next few weeks: Montelupone, nestled in the Macerate province in the Marche region on the east coast of Italy.

Sofia lived with her thirteen-year-old sister Giovanna, her mother Rosa and her grandparents, Giulia and Giuseppe. They all lived in one wonderful big house on the edge of the village. No sooner as I had arrived, Rosa and Giulia had led me to the family dining room and urged me with their hands to sit down before disappearing to the kitchen.

Eating was no hurried affair and lunch took well over an hour, with the main meal being followed by fresh fruits from the garden. The family didn't gulp their food down nor glance at watches or the TV that sat on the unit under the lazy fan. It was just another piece of furniture, a background noise. Instead, they spoke to one another and I was fascinated with their interaction.

Occasionally, Alessandro would stop eating, placing his cutlery down just so he could emphasise his story with his hands. I saw the way he looked at Rosa, with deep admiration. When she placed food on the table, he would wrap his arm around her aproned waist and pull her towards him; a gesture refuted as she smiled and muttered, releasing his embrace. It was clear that he idolised his two daughters too – when they spoke, he would smile and his dark eyes danced with pride and fatherly love.

After lunch, Alessandro returned to work and Rosa and Giulia disappeared back to the kitchen to wash up and prepare for the next feast that evening. It was their private domain. At least that's how it appeared; I rarely saw the food magic happening inside the kitchen hidden behind the large wooden doors. Just once I witnessed Rosa making gnocchi from scratch on a worn-out wooden block. She made everything by hand – even the pasta.

Sofia led me to our room; a large wooden door opened onto marble tiled floors. The room was dark and pleasantly cool. There were two single beds, belonging to the girls and a camp bed made up at the other side of the large room, presumably for me.

Sophia walked over to the large window shrouded in darkness, the heavy shutters closed across it. "Look ... come," she said, stretching out her hand for me to join her as she unbolted the wooden shutters and pushed them outwards. The once-dark room flooded with bright sunlight and an explosion of dust danced in shafts of the brilliant beams.

The girls' room was on the high side of the house at the edge of the village, so beyond the Juliet balcony was a sheer drop that fell away to the garden below, a space that belonged to Giuseppe.

The shutters clattered against the house walls and Giuseppe looked up – he was beneath the steep house walls in his garden, tending to a handful of chickens. Their coop sat amongst a busy collection of shrubs and herbs, dotted with fruit and lemon trees. I'd never seen a real lemon tree before. Lemons came from supermarkets; I'd never considered they grew in people's gardens.

But beyond the garden wall lay the most breathtaking view: fields of bright yellow sunflowers in full bloom; gently wavering gold and green met other fields of the same, creating a golden patchwork of colour, sectioned only by lines of trees and little brick houses on the horizon. The sky was perfectly blue with just a scattering of wispy white clouds.

I gasped at the scene before me. I wanted to cry. I wanted to paint this landscape and capture this moment forever, just for me. I'd never seen anything so beautiful, so idyllic. So romantic.

It was a far cry from the bedroom view that I'd shared with Sofia a few months earlier: grey pebble-dashed walls on cloned houses under dull cloudy skies; cars and double-decker buses and chewing-gummed pavements. I'd never seen anything other than the greys of England's cities and skies, or the rolling green hills of Ireland, but this was a whole new part of nature's paint palette. This picture-postcard landscape was my view for the next six weeks.

The house was large and airy and the shuttered windows were kept firmly bolted during the heat of the day, helping to keep the marbled floor cool underfoot. There was a family room with dark wooden furniture and leather sofas, but I only ever saw it once – on the first tour of the house. It seemed most of the family's life centred around the large dining room with its food and conversation.

Rosa would mop the marble floors throughout the house early every morning, before preparing lunch. She was a warm, motherly woman with a kind face. Sometimes she would come and stroke my cheek as she softly spoke to me in Italian. I had no idea of her words' meaning but I knew from the way she touched my face tenderly that she saw a fifteen-year-old girl in a different country far away from her mother, a little lost. It was her way of soothing me and it helped. I missed Mum. She was all I'd ever known. She was my comfort. I missed John too.

Sophia, Giovanna and the other girls in the village all seemed to dress similarly, despite the variation in their body shape. Some of the girls the same age as me had generous curves, ones they didn't appear to be ashamed of. They all wore denim jeans, white T-shirts and brown leather brogues. They looked casual, but smart. They didn't deliberately drown their bodies in clothes, they unintentionally accentuated their shapes in tighter fits. I wanted to be like them. I wanted to feel more at ease in my body again. It had been so long I'd forgotten what it felt like.

I bought two pairs of brogues, one brown leather pair and one burgundy pair from the local street market with my spending money. I rolled my jeans up a couple of times so you could see my ankles and pale skin. At least it made me look taller. I wore my brogue shoes sockless, just like the other girls. And I wore the same white shirts day after day. I didn't need to show my arms like the others, but that way at least I felt like I fitted in.

No one ate breakfast in Sofia's house – they just drank a large cup of black coffee and sometimes ate a slice of very dry-looking cake. I passed on both. But the lunch and dinners were grand food affairs twice a day. Each sitting lasting over an hour and I began to adjust to these gastronomical events.

Dinner was around 8pm and even more leisurely than lunch as Alessandro had finished work for the day. I noticed Sofia's family never ate dessert, not in the way I had known whilst growing up. Instead, Giuseppe would bring a bowl of fresh apricots to the table that he had picked that day from the generous gardens. He and Alessandro would sit on the edge between debate and arguing, slicing pieces of the fruit until they reached the stones inside. They would drop the slices of fruit into their wine and swirl them about with practiced ease, infusing the fruit. Once they had finished drinking their wine, they would scoop the fruit out and savour it. It was their dessert. Everything from the wine they drank to the chicken they ate was homegrown, including the herbs and olive oil that dressed them.

Sofia would excuse us from the table at around 10pm and, despite my attempts to help wash dishes, Rosa would dismiss me with a wave of her hands. Each night, we would walk the short distance through the winding streets to the piazza for gelato. The *Piazza del Comune* was a stone square built around a fourteen-century priory, gently lit up at night. It sat under the shadow of *Palazzo del Podesta* tower. Under its five stone archways was an area where the young people of the town would all gather after their family dinners at night and sit and chat.

I'd sit under there observing their passionate exchanges, my stare sometimes drifting to the elderly gentlemen who sat beyond on the opposite side of the piazza at little tables, some playing board games and bickering whilst others sipped espresso served from the little gelato shop.

The setting was so removed from my homelife. So alien and different yet utterly captivating. The warm summer evenings only served to intensify the enchanting location. It was a place that stirred me in a way I'd never felt.

The local boys were fascinated with me, the thin, pale girl with the blue eyes, and I was equally fascinated by them. They looked like the men from movies – tanned with big smiles, full of laughter and passionate conversation with a rich Italian accent. The language was beautiful, it rolled off their tongues with a sweetly melodic rhythm. I was mesmerised by the way they spoke and the way they moved their svelte bodies in playful tussles.

Lorenzo, a boy of seventeen, took a particular shine to me.

Lorenzo had warm dark eyes and thick brown curls that framed his face. He wore several leather bracelets on his wrists and one woven white one that stood out and highlighted his golden skin. Every night he would sit nearby, watching me – an intense stare he would barely blink from and I would shift uncomfortably on the stone bench. It felt as if he was peeling back my clothes with his eyes from afar, without a single touch and I danced between delicious butterflies and embarrassment.

Does he fancy me, even at this weight? I wondered.

"*Sei un piccolo fiore Inglese* [You are a small English flower]" Lorenzo whispered. "Emilee, you are ... how you say it ... small ... sweet? *Bella* [beautiful]. I made this for you. Can you wear it?"

Lorenzo gently lifted my wrist and tied a red cotton friendship bracelet around it. I offered my arm willingly, staring at his beautiful dark eyes. I could feel my cheeks flushing as I squirmed a little on the wall.

"*Per te mio dolce amore* [for you my sweet love]." He smiled and touched my hand before taking his place back on the wall.

After a week of silent observation, Lorenzo was softly wooing me and I felt myself falling into a dreamlike dizziness around him despite John back at home. I'd never been wooed. I'd been chatted up, ridiculed by boys and kissed by John, but never wooed.

The Italian boys enjoyed practicing their English skills on me and took great delight in teaching me some Italian phrases in return. It was mostly profanities and sexual innuendo which they would get me to repeat awkwardly, then fall about laughing at my rude repetitions and gullibility.

"Vieni con me tra i cespugli! [Come with me into the bushes!]" I'd repeat. It sounded so much more glamorous than the crude invitation it was.

The Italian boys were different to my English friends, they

played affectionately with each other and they showed a general interest in me, keen to learn about English culture and language. They didn't say I was too skinny or too pale and didn't tell me I was frigid – well, I don't think they did. I was happy in my oblivion to the meaning of their words and bathed in their interest in me.

I'd parted from John with the promise of sending him weekly letters. They were to be our only means of contact. True to my word, I wrote John long love letters every week, telling him of my adventures, censoring some parts – Lorenzo, mostly. Each week I posted them at the little grocery shop in one of the side roads of the main piazza that doubled as a post office.

I settled into my new way of life and the warm summer days rolled by. Sofia and the rest of the youth of the town were on summer break, so we spent our days altogether exploring the town, hanging out in the shade of the municipal building, eating gelato.

One Tuesday afternoon, Sofia, Giovanna and I, along with a large group of the other kids, caught the town bus to Portonova beach. As they hopped off the bus, hot and bothered and full of enthusiasm for a cooling swim, I reluctantly followed. Once the towels were thrown on the sand, the boys began to strip off, pulling their tops off to reveal young men's bodies in the making.

"*Andiamo, avanti!*" they cheered as they raced across the hot sand towards the glistening Adriatic Sea.

The girls were gossiping as they disrobed to reveal colourful bikinis and underarm hair. It was the first time I had seen girls with body hair. It was oddly curious to me – I'd only known underarm or leg hair as almost forbidden, somehow taboo, and had always shaved mine. Maybe they viewed my shaved armpits as equally curious?

I lay on my towel fully clothed. Underneath my T-shirt and jeans, I sweltered in the hot June sunshine. As much as I wanted to fit in, I had not undressed publicly since the doctor's office almost a year before. And that was just in front of Mum and one man. This was different. These were my peers, these girls and boys who I sat with night after night, chatting and laughing. They only knew me as fully dressed Emily; they liked the clothed version of me. Would they still like the me underneath my clothes?

I'd sat next to Lorenzo whilst riding the bus to the beach and been distracted from my discomfort, but there, as I sat on the beach, the reality hit me. If I wanted to blend in, I would have to strip down to the bikini I was wearing underneath. The thought of undressing so publicly filled me with overwhelming anxiety but a pale English girl sitting fully clothed on a beach in scorching sunshine *really* stood out.

I felt sick. It was hard to breathe.

Why did I agree to come here? I asked myself.

"Come, Emily, come swimming with us." Sofia held her hand out towards me, encouraging me. The other girls were already standing up, waiting to go.

I wriggled out of my jeans, resuming my position on my tummy on the towel, before stripping off my shirt. I had virgin-white skin – the closest it had ever been to the sun was the logo on a bottle of fake tan. I felt naked, exposed in just my green and white polka-dot bikini. Without the protection of clothes, my skin crawled.

I pushed myself up and sat with my back to the sun, pulling my T-shirt over me knowing that if I didn't, I would be nursing sunburn later that night. I knew I stood out – my skin iridescent next to the tanned, dark-haired Italian girls. I felt them watching me rub in the sunscreen to my arms and legs. I was grateful the boys, including Lorenzo, were already frolicking in the waves, oblivious to my near-nakedness on the beach.

It was the most exposed and uncomfortable I had felt since anorexia had taken over my mind and body but I had so wanted to fit in, to be a cast member of this make-believe film set with the gorgeous Italian teens who played their parts so effortlessly. The more I avoided stripping off, the more attention I was drawing to myself.

Alexandria, one of the girls who had been on the bus with us, pulled a friend towards her and they both stood staring at me.

"*Schifoso,*" the girl whispered to Alexandria, a word I later found out meant 'disgusting'. She was looking at me as she spoke and her face said it clearly. I knew from her expression and tone it wasn't a compliment. She was a mean girl.

I pulled my shirt back on and down to my bottom, drawing my knees together. The less flesh on show, the better.

"I think I will stay here – you go!" I called out to Sofia, who was chattering and oblivious to the mean girl's comment.

I lay on the beach half-dressed with my towel covering my bare legs, watching the rest of the cast splash and swim and stay cool in the hot Italian sunshine as I turned redder and sweated under a sunscreen layer and too many clothes. I waited until they were playing volleyball on the sand to pull my jeans back on as fast as I could.

Good, no one else saw me, I told myself, relieved.

I scooped up the hot, dry sand next to me with my hand, letting it run through my fingers and watching it fall into a gentle mound. I hated myself. Why couldn't I just fit in?

After a couple of hours, everyone dressed and headed for the bus home to Montelupone in time for dinner. The sun was still bathing the village in warm, golden light and despite the safety of my sunscreen and clothes all day, my skin was glowing red and uncomfortably hot.

The family are gathered for dinner around the heavy wooden table, the fan rhythmically whirling above our heads but making no difference to the July evening air. It is uncomfortably hot. The TV is playing Italian adverts. Now I recognise many of them and I no longer dread these dinners. I am no longer the eating freak show, I am a part of the family now.

Rosa carries a large rectangular tray to the table and sets it down in front of me. Nestled in the baking tray is the largest pizza I have ever seen, its thin outer crust dusted in tiny golden grains like sand, with circles of white cheese melted in puddles on top of rich crimson sauce, crowned by torn bright green leaves.

Real pizza. I have never eaten *real* pizza before. It smells delicious. I am salivating and this time, I can eat it.

"*Buon Compleanno!*" Rosa claps her hands as she wishes me happy birthday and the family join in.

"*Si, si – Buon Compleanno!*" they chorus together.

I smile. "*Grazie a tutti.*"

It's taken me almost six weeks to be brave enough to utter a few words to this beautiful family in their native tongue.

"Ahh, *bravo bravo, excellente*!" Alessandro applauds me and his family echo him. "Bravo!"

My Italian adventure was ending. My sixteenth birthday was during my last week in Italy and that night we ate Rosa's delicious pizza for dinner followed by her tiramisu, a celebratory meal made especially for the English birthday girl. After dinner we wandered to the piazza, one final time for me.

"Ecco, Emily, Buon Compleanno!" A small crowd of my newfound friends clapped as they greeted me. I was centre of attention, but this time it felt almost comforting; celebratory and uplifting, not overwhelming.

I sat on the stone bench, knowing it was my last night. Part of me didn't want to leave this place. I'd made new friends; I'd unknowingly declared a truce in my battle with food. Aside from the beach incident near the beginning, for the most part I had viewed my body a little differently too, through softer, much kinder lenses.

And someone had fallen for me, even though I wasn't really thin anymore. And maybe I had fallen for him a little too.

Lorenzo looked at me sadly as he passed me a folded piece of paper with his address written on it. "*Mi mancherai il mio fiore inglese. Devi scrivermi.* [I will miss you my English flower. You must write to me]. I miss you when you go from Italy, we can write together, yes?"

I could have listened to his voice forever. That soft velvet voice and Italian accent coating his broken English. "Um ... yes, I suppose," I stutter shyly. "Thank you. I mean ... *grazie,* Lorenzo."

Lorenzo leant forward and hugged me, a little awkwardly but long enough for me to feel his warmth and smell his skin. The faint smell of a boyish cologne was every bit as delicious as I had imagined it to be.

He grinned. "*Ciao, bella.*"

"*Ciao*, Lorenzo."

FAILED

AUGUST 1988

THE NEXT DAY I FLEW BACK HOME TO ENGLAND. I'D SPENT six wonderful weeks fully immersed in Italian life in Montelupone, bathing in the warm Italian sunshine with a large, loving family who spent time altogether. I'd been welcomed by a family of strangers, cared for and treated like another daughter. I left them in tears knowing I'd probably never see them again, despite our best intentions of staying in touch by letter.

"Jesus, you're looking well, Emily." Mum beamed as she met me at the airport. I could see her relief. "It's good to have you home, love." She threw her arms around me and squeezed me tightly.

I had a splattering of freckles and faint colour and although she never said a word, I knew she was relieved the six weeks of pasta, gelato and pizza had paid off for her, if not for me.

Everything at home was the same: my family life, John, my house, but I was different. Something had moved within me. I'd seen another life; I'd lived and breathed a different culture; I'd starred in a romance film of my own making, daydreaming a different reality, one featuring warm sunshine, beautiful scenery, carefree summer nights and a make-believe love with a beautiful Italian boy. Everything at home felt grey and harsh by comparison and it was unsettling.

I had eaten much more freely in Italy. As the weeks had rolled on there, I became accustomed to eating regularly and food was paired with pleasure. It had been quietly healing for me. I tapped into a sense of happiness in Italy and I felt peaceful. When I returned, I could feel myself sinking a little. I became once again very much more self-conscious of my body. The calorie obsession crept back in. It had just been interrupted and temporarily silenced by a change of scene.

Just before I left for Italy, I'd applied for the local art college and an interview was scheduled for a couple of weeks after my return. Art had become my favourite lesson at school during the previous couple of years. It was within my art that I could lose myself for hours. Sometimes I'd pack up a sketchpad and watercolour set and catch a bus to the beach, where I would sit alone and paint the wintry landscapes. I was often teased by my friends. They had all moved on with boyfriends, smoking, cider and parties, yet that held no appeal to me. Drinking was out of the question – I feared being drunk; I feared losing control. Instead, I filled my time painting. I was a loner and I enjoyed it that way.

John played football every weekend which gave me an excuse to isolate and paint. Sometimes I'd go to the beach and search for flotsam – odd items that would wash up on the beach. Seaweed, rope, weathered glass were junk to most, but they held a fascination to me with their seaworn textures and tangled clutter. I'd buy a cheap hot chocolate from the local burger bar, never to drink it but to warm my hands from the biting winter cold, then I'd sit and sketch my beach treasure. I progressed to fine-art drawing with ink pens and drifted away from painting –

a pen and pocketbook was easier to carry and more inconspicuous to passers-by at the beach.

I left school with an A-plus in art – the highest in my year, despite my lack of confidence in my own ability and applied for a course in natural-history illustration at the local art college. Armed with my portfolio and sketch books, I headed to my interview with an air of quiet confidence at my A grade and catalogue of illustrations of shells and flowers. I didn't once doubt I would get a place on the course. I'd heard that my old school friend, Kerry, had been accepted on a fashion course there.

A couple of weeks later, I received a letter from the college. Unfortunately, at sixteen, I was considered too young for the course. It was more suited to a more mature candidate with a more extensive portfolio in natural-history illustration. I had failed to get in. It was my first official knockback and confirmed to me what I already believed: that I wasn't good enough. That week I packed up my pens, paints, pencils and sketchpad and vowed never to touch them again. Two weeks later I got myself a job in a card shop selling greetings cards.

STEPPING INTO MUM'S SHOES

AUGUST 1989

"I CAN SEE YOUR TITS."

A man in his late fifties is sitting in front of me, or maybe he's younger. It's hard to tell. He shoves some paperwork under the metal grill. It smells of damp and fags.

"How can I help you today, sir?"

He leers at me. I try to ignore the comment and carry on reading his form.

I wonder if he can hear my heart racing behind this bra?

I feel a little scared. Humiliated. My cheeks are burning red.

"What's your name and current address please, sir?"

"Hey, I *said* I can see your tits." He slaps his lips together in a fake kiss. "Do you want to meet me outside after you finish work? I'd give you a good seeing to!" He laughs and the smell of his whisky-soaked breath cannot be held back by a glass screen or metal grill.

My skin crawls under my uniform shirt. He can't touch me but I feel dirty, violated.

Please get me out of here.

Just after my seventeenth birthday, I started working for the local government benefits office. Mum had applied for the job in my name without me knowing, having seen an advert in the local paper. She thought a solid government job would settle me down after my college disappointment. Mum was also concerned the discontent might send me spiralling back towards the eating disorder.

I survived the interview, masking my nerves enough to impress the panel of three suited civil servants in their stuffy high-rise office. The following month I started working in a job that would introduce me to the depravity of human life in many forms, a job where I saw things, I wish I never had.

My job was to sit behind glass screens with metal grills and listen to people ask, often beg, shout and scream, for money and then try to placate them when they lost their heads in angry desperation. At seventeen, I wasn't emotionally equipped to cope with alcoholism, drug abuse, mental illness and the often-volatile behaviours that accompanied people at their lowest ebb in life. The job utterly terrified me and I dreaded it each day, yet felt grateful to least be earning a reasonable wage in a secure job at a time when the country was heading into recession.

I never got used to the sound of shouting or the verbal abuse directed at me. But the thing I found the hardest to endure were the creeps who'd comment on the size of my seventeen-year-old breasts, my bra visible under my white uniform shirt, my seventeen-year-old body and their grubby minds imagining what they like to do to me – sometimes unashamedly sharing their desires with me. Then there were the men who stroked my fingers when I passed the forms under the grill for signing, a dirty smile in their eyes, licking their lips in gratification. I even had a stalker who wrote me love letters and smashed the glass screen when I didn't oblige his twisted invitations. I hated the job but I tolerated it because I didn't know I could do any better.

I had been dating John for two years when Mum moved back to Ireland with Dave to care for my elderly grandparents. Dave also wanted land to keep horses. He had dreams and he swept Mum up in them. I refused to go and chose to stay with John, my man – well, a boy really, who still loved me at the size I was, despite my weight gain. He was someone who wanted to love me and stick around, who wouldn't leave me or let me down. I lost myself in him and isolated myself entirely from my friends.

I moved in with Ryan and John into a flat owned by Dave, in a less-than-desirable area of town, within walking distance of my workplace. It was a frightening transition from the family home, but my exposure to gritty life at work had prepared me for most things.

Mum was grateful I had the watchful eye of Ryan and John when she left, but the reality was very different. I was the one keeping an eye on Ryan instead, cooking dinners for him and John. They neither asked nor expected it from me, but I took on the role willingly. It gave me a purpose and nurturing these men and garnering their approval made me feel useful. It made me feel wanted.

"Here we go!" I placed a large roast dinner on the table in front of John and Ryan. There were mountains of roast potatoes and Yorkshire puddings piled high with chicken, stuffing and broccoli, all of it swimming in gravy.

"Thanks, Emily, this looks great. I'm starving!" Ryan rubbed his hands together in anticipation of a good feed.

"Thanks, love," John echoed.

I sat next to them both with a small helping watching,

waiting for their acknowledgment. I'd only just learnt how to cook roast dinners like Mum.

"Mmm, it's really good, Emily." Ryan smiled through a mouthful of potatoes and gravy.

I relaxed, smiling. There was something oddly pleasurable about watching them eat the piles of food I gave them. I didn't have to eat it myself, but it still satisfied me.

It's a win, win, Emily, I told myself. *All the pleasure of food without the calories.*

Now I could eat mine, just a little: two potatoes, one slice of chicken and a mouthful of broccoli drizzled with gravy.

I was watching my food intake again.

DARE TO BARE

AUGUST 1990

When John and I went food shopping, I felt compelled to inspect food for fat content and calories. Despite being able to eat a more normalised diet, I continued to avoid the 'bad' foods I'd first given up at thirteen. Cakes, chocolate and crisps were permanently banned. I always went for the lowest-fat version of everything: yogurt, milk, meat, cheese. Sometimes, food shopping could take ninety minutes, most of that time consumed with my meticulous studying of food labels.

In 1990, we enjoyed a particularly warm summer in England. Despite being what one would consider within a normal weight range by then, I still covered my body up. I struggled to show my arms or legs, feeling both were still overweight and unsightly. I didn't have the magazine-quality tanned skin. I had pale, mottled skin; it looked almost blue when cold and had a lumpy, rough, pimpled texture resembling corned beef fresh out of a can.

It was a time when fake tanning creams still turned your skin absurdly orange and streaky and the pungent smell gave away your tanning attempts if the glaring orange glow-up hadn't already done the job. Like many other young women, I wanted tanned skin, so it was under a reassuring dark-orange fake tan, I challenged myself to wearing a sleeveless top and shorts to walk to the local shops on a beautifully sunny August afternoon.

I'd just had my long hair (already curly) spiral-permed for extra volume and had backcombed the front into a fashionable height, fixed in place with cement-like hairspray. I was a picture of early nineties' elegance. For the first time in years, I felt brave enough to walk outside the front door half-dressed.

Okay, Emily, you can do this, I told myself. *Breathe.*

My heart was racing.

I approached an antique shop that had always fascinated me when walking past it on my way to work every day. I would often pause to peek in at its eclectic collection of oddities in the window, the kind of things I used to love to sketch – each object whispered something of its mystical history.

There, standing propped up against the shop doorway was the owner, smoking casually as he bathed in the warm sunshine with his highlighted blond hair sashaying over his shoulders. (Golden highlighted hair was the in-thing back then.) I noticed this tanned Adonis from afar, despite his obvious decade in age on me.

He smiled, winking at me as I approached and our eyes met.

Oh no, ground open up and swallow me, please, I thought.

"Lovely weather today, isn't it?" he remarked coolly, exhaling a long line of smoke into the air. He glanced at my legs and I watched his eyes travel up my body, over my breasts to my eyes. Mr Cool smiled, a grin I'd seen before, though much less predatory than some I'd encountered at work.

"Um ... er ... yes," I replied awkwardly.

My legs felt weak and my heart thumped loudly behind my barely-a-B-cup bra. Here was an older man flirting with me and as I passed, I felt his stare on my behind. My stomach flipped at his attention, but not in a nice, butterfly way. Inside, I was cringeing.

My legs, they look fat, don't they? my inner voice said. *My arms are fat. This is awful. Why did I come out dressed like this?!*

It was the one and only time I wore shorts in the UK as a young woman.

Just after my nineteenth birthday, John and I decided to go on our first holiday together to Kalymnos, a remote Greek island off the island of Kos. I had never fully exposed my body to the sun before, not since early childhood, and it felt good. To feel real warmth on my bare skin was a new and unfamiliar feeling.

We'd slather our bodies in cheap, oily sunscreen and lie on the beach for hours at a time. It offered the lowest sun-protection possible. In our naivety, we believed the lower the factor, the better your tan would be. John had swarthy skin that tanned deep-brown easily. I just turned fifty shades of red and fried.

We were surrounded by people on the beach: people I didn't know, who I would never see again and that anonymity felt reassuring. It was the first time I felt safe revealing my body. Somehow showing more flesh in a bikini in front of strangers with John by my side felt less exposing than showing my arms and legs at home to people I saw regularly.

EXERCISE, DEFICIT, CONTROL

OCTOBER 1991

A COUPLE OF YEARS AFTER MUM LEFT ENGLAND, THINGS began to really sour in her marriage. Dave's gambling habits had caught up with him and he was in debt – pulling Mum into them along with him. His aggressive behaviour accelerated dangerously and Mum no longer felt safe in the same house as him. She escaped him and went into hiding in Belfast and Dave wasn't game enough to try and find her.

Dave returned to the UK and began to pay unannounced visits to Ryan, John and me. He saw us as a route to contact my mum who wanted nothing to do with him. We had no choice but to see him; he was coming round each month to collect the rent money from us.

A few months after his return, he appeared one day and told us we had a fortnight to leave his flat. Dave said it was being repossessed by the bank due to the recession. In fact, he had been using the rent money to gamble rather than pay the mortgage. The bank foreclosed and we were left homeless. I had no family left locally so John and I moved into his parents' dining room and slept on camp beds – there was nowhere else left to go.

Within three months, Ryan bought his first home, a top-floor flat with three bedrooms, so there was room for John and me. Life continued much as it had and I continued to care for my brother and John. I was back in the area I'd spent my teenage years in, so there was some comfort in the familiarity, though it was hard to pass the home my mum sold to move to Ireland. Although it wasn't always the easiest home to live in, it was where I was last with my mum and I missed her terribly.

My life felt uncertain, I had no real direction and that unsettled me. I slowly became more vigilant about my weight and food intake. I was controlling the only thing I could – calories – and before long, how many I could burn. It began with an aerobics class in the local school hall. Once a week to begin with, but that soon crept up to two plus swimming laps at the local pool. Then I added in daily sessions on Ryan's treadmill. I *hated* exercise, it always felt like punishment – something to be endured. But the reward was always waiting at the end of every session – a guaranteed calorie deficit.

DOWN UNDER

JANUARY 1993

I'M STANDING AT THE ENTRANCE OF THE FOOD MALL. I don't know where to look first, where to begin. I've never seen so much food.

Piles of golden nachos bathed in sour cream and half a pound of cheese melting in.

Creamy pastas and potato wedges in giant silver dishes.

Fries stacked in crisscross batches.

Garlic bread dripping in butter and warm curries, glistening with ghee.

Chinese buffets: noodles and fried chicken all sit in huge mounds.

Colourful food pyramids sit under warm yellow lights.

The steam is rising and the smells are mixing, pulling me in.

"Come on honey, let's go in." Dad puts his arm around me, ushering me into the mall.

On my twenty-first birthday, my dad, who had been living in Australia for many years, gifted me a plane ticket to visit him.

I'd not seen him for several years, but John was excited at the prospect of a holiday, so we saved for a few months for his airfare. In January 1993, we flew to Perth and left behind the dismal weather and long dark nights of an English winter.

My reunion with my dad was a little uncomfortable. We were unfamiliar with each other, but I was keen to introduce him to John and excited to explore Western Australia. I set my awkwardness aside and bathed in my dad's obvious pride in me. Wanting to impress John and I, he'd planned outings and excursions every day and seemed to quietly revel in the introductions he made to his small group of friends and musical acquaintances.

"This is my daughter, Emily," he'd say proudly, arm around my waist, squeezing me tightly.

I think he wanted to claim me as his after so many years living a solitary life. Likewise, I'd wanted to be noticed and held by my dad my whole life, to be acknowledged as his daughter. We had the best intentions, but somehow our reunion felt a little strained.

Despite the awkwardness between us, John and I enjoyed three sun-soaked weeks exploring Western Australia with my dad. He introduced John and I to the shopping malls with their giant food courts. It was a wonderful trip in every way and as our last day approached, I realised I'd opened my heart to him. I'd given myself permission to be vulnerable again, to be his little girl and enjoy his pride in me, his compliments at how well I'd turned out, how I had a respectable job and a decent man. I sought his approval daily and got it; it was satisfying something deep inside me. For three weeks he temporarily filled a void he'd left in my life for twenty-one years.

Despite that, there was an unspoken oddness between us, as if we were still strangers. I still couldn't call him Dad – it seemed unnatural to. But I had, on some level, reconnected with him as the time approached to say goodbye to him all over again.

Australia is 9,000 miles away from England. In 1993, there was no internet or video-calling. I knew neither of us would be travelling anytime soon. As we boarded our long flight home; I realised I was really going to miss him.

Within a few weeks of returning from Australia, one of Ryan's friends was chatting to John and me about our recent holiday and asked us if we could ever consider living there. It was a question we had never asked ourselves, or each other, but his query planted a seed of interest within us both. We lived in a room in a shared house, with no real roots or money behind us. I was stuck in a frightening job I hated and I was dealing with an obsession with what I ate and how much I weighed. John worked outdoors on a farm through the harsh winters. It didn't feel like we had much to lose or leave behind. Australia had given us both a taste of an alternative life, one that promised sunshine, a home of our own, maybe even a swimming pool. And it promised me a relationship with my dad.

Within months, John and I applied to emigrate to Australia – it was a lengthy process that required medical tests and form filling and hefty fees. It also required us to prove our relationship status. The easiest way was to get married.

I'm standing in front of the hotel dressing-room mirror, staring at my reflection.

My face looks so round.

I just don't understand it. I've been so careful on this diet. I've been watching *everything* I eat. I walked for ages on the treadmill every day. It wasn't enough though, clearly.

You blew it, Emily.

My cheeks are burning red under all this foundation. They look so ugly. My chest feels tight and my heart is racing – I'm struggling to stay calm.

Will John still think I look pretty enough for him?

Mum is standing behind me stroking my hair, in tears. Her little girl is now a bride-to-be.

The wedding will take me far away from her, but it is one that offers me a new beginning, away from all this worry about food and my body.

She stayed with me last night. We lay beside each other sharing stories and laughing, just like we did when I was a kid. She did my hair for me. She helped me with my make-up too. Simple, special moments between us I will quietly treasure.

Do you know how much I love you, Mum? I'm sorry I never tell you.

"Emily ... my beautiful wee princess." She smiles through her tears, smoothing down my wispy curls, trying their best to escape the hairspray.

I don't feel like one, Mum.

I look different to how I imagined I would today. I don't feel beautiful like the women in the bridal magazines. I feel home-made and put together with burning red, round cheeks.

I stare at the bride in the mirror, disappointed in her. She didn't try hard enough. Shes *still* not thin.

My dress feels tight around my middle, it's hard to breathe.

Pull the sleeves down a bit lower. Your arms are fat.

I turn to the side.

Urgh, your belly sticks out, Emily.

I look away.

"Emily, the car is here, come on love, we have to leave..."

Three months later, John and I married at the local registry office. I invited my dad to give me away to John, but he couldn't come back. Work commitments and 9,000 miles got in the way. It hurt a little. This was what dads were *supposed* to do – give their daughters away at their weddings. Instead, Mum flew back from Ireland and gave me away to John. It was a simple wedding, a means to an end, but it allowed our families to send us off with a celebration.

In September 1994, John and I emigrated to Perth. As heartbreaking as it was to leave Mum and Ryan behind, I felt optimistic. It felt like a clean slate, a chance to leave my old life behind.

Twenty-four hours later and one brief stopover, we landed in Australia and my dad was standing waiting for me in the arrivals lounge of Perth Airport, a big smile across his face and holding a little stuffed koala with an Australian flag for his little girl. It was time to welcome his daughter to the place he called home.

"Honey, can you stop leaving dishes in the sink? I like to wash up as I go," Dad reminds me.

"Oh sorry, I was going to do them later," I counter, just a little wounded.

"Can you stop leaving wet towels in the bathroom, hang them outside to dry, honey?"

"Oh, sorry, yeah of course."

"Emily, can you put that rubbish straight out in the bin?"

"What's that stain on the carpet? Did you spill something?"

What am I, a child?

"Maybe you and John could start looking for somewhere else to live."

John and I lived with my dad for six months. It wasn't an easy adjustment for any of us. We both secured work within the first week of landing, but in essence we were all strangers and my dad had lived alone for over ten years, so it took some time for us all to settle. Trivial things I did, or didn't do in the way my dad wanted, were getting under his skin and I rebelled against his criticism of me, taking it very personally.

The big elephant in the room remained; an elephant fattened up by years of separation from each other and little contact. I still couldn't call him dad, even after all those years. So, I called him nothing. I know he noticed. I know it hurt. His eyes told me, yet still I couldn't force the word out. He remained nameless to me.

After six months living together, we had all had enough of each other and John and I moved into a rental property. Moving out gave us all a chance to breathe and time to search for our first home. It also gave my relationship with my dad the space to heal and grow.

Within a year, we bought our first home, a small bungalow that needed updating, but its biggest draw was its garden and swimming pool. Despite the heat in Australia, I still couldn't show my body to anyone – specially my limbs, they were overweight and ugly to me.

I'd been warned by my doctor before I left the UK that I was moving to the worst possible place in the world for my pale skin, now covered in moles of various sizes. Moles were a genetic gift from my parents. I'd had two removed before leaving the UK – my three holidays in the Greek islands with factor-two oil and customary sunburn had gifted me sun-damaged skin and a couple of suspect moles amongst my collection. Post-op, the doctor warned me to always keep myself covered up in Australia.

Great! That's suits me, I decided. I didn't need any excuses to hide my body away, but the doctors warning legitimised my desire to cover it up. I would only swim in a full-body swimsuit and kept my arms and legs covered up all the time.

We lived a ten-minute walk from a large shopping mall in Perth with a food hall that served over a dozen or so international cuisines: Mexican fajitas, Chinese buffets, Indian curries and Australian barbecues, all for a few dollars. Apart from dipping my toes in traditional Italian food in Italy, the most adventurous food I had tried was a jacket potato from a local takeaway once. I had never been to a shopping mall before my holiday to Australia, let alone seen a food hall. The mall offered air-conditioned respite from the relentless Australian heat. The food hall offered fast and tasty food which was an easy solution for a quick dinner whilst we renovated the kitchen.

Having come from England where takeaways were still scarce, especially for a family of eight, this seemed like gastronomical heaven to John. After years of restriction, I now gave myself permission.

"Emily, try this."

Dad places a brown paper bag down on the table next to me after a feed.

"Thanks. What is it?"

"It's a blueberry muffin. I think you'll like this." He smiles.

I open the bag and that familiar and distinct smell of fresh cake hits my nose. I pull the muffin out – it's huge, as big as my fist. I tear off the muffin top coated in a generous layer of sweet cream cheese, revealing plump purple berries bursting with flavour and juice underneath. I push it in my mouth.

I've missed this.

The slightly chewy, crunchy muffin lid melts in my mouth. The blueberries are sweet. It's gone in minutes. I press my finger into the empty muffin case to gather up every last crumb.

"See, I told you you'd like it," Dad says.

Dad discovered through conversation how much I had loved Mum's cakes as a child and just outside the food mall was a muffin shop. Once he realised how much I enjoyed the first muffin, he often brought them to me: a sweet surprise two or three times a week.

That introduction to the food court on holiday was the first time I'd really sat down and eaten with my dad. Now we were doing it several times a week and I enjoyed sharing mealtimes with him. My dad had also found his appetite. He rarely ate in the day, but he could demolish a huge plate of food in the evening and several bottles of beer afterwards.

Dad, John and I would pile our plates high with mounds of exotic deliciousness. I'm not sure if the 'all you can eat' mentality is reserved for just a few people or if everyone feels the same – duty-bound to pile as much food as possible onto your plate, maximising value for money. We all seemed compelled to load up our plates and because our eyes were far bigger than our bellies we would often struggle to finish that night's offerings. This went on for almost twelve weeks – nightly visits to the food hall, interspersed with the odd barbecue in the backyard.

The food, although fresh, wasn't exactly healthy. Or maybe it was and I just avoided the healthy options like sushi and headed straight for the carb-loaded, cheese-covered calorific mountains. These were all things I'd never tried or certainly never indulged in any vast quantities. These foods were mostly ones I had forbidden for many years. I always chose meals loaded with salt and fat – the two things that made them taste ... well, so good!

Not having a functioning kitchen during that time granted us permission to nip over the road after a long day at work and fill up on cheap, fattening food. During the same period, John bought me a novelty chocolate bar as one of my birthday gifts. This was no ordinary chocolate bar – it weighed 2kg. I managed to eat it all in under two weeks.

I had not eaten chocolate for years; it had been promoted to the top of the 'bad food' league years before, but something changed when I moved to Australia. For the first time in years, I suppose I felt truly content. We had a new and exciting life in our home in the sun. John loved me just as I was and finally my dad was a part of my life and wanting to spend time with me. Both the men in my life wanted to please me and they discovered food gave me pleasure. Unfortunately, so had I.

Nearing the end of our house renovations, I remember going to the doctor with out-of-character headaches. The doctor ran some blood tests and routinely weighed me. I had gained twenty-one pounds in just a few months and my blood pressure was elevated. A few days later I went back to get my blood results. My cholesterol levels were far too high for a young woman aged twenty-four.

The doctor confirmed the high-fat diet I was indulging in, including the consumption of the enormous chocolate bar, had probably raised my cholesterol levels and a lifestyle overhaul was necessary. He was confident I could reduce my cholesterol through diet and exercise.

That young Aussie doctor said something to me that day

that has sat with me for twenty-five years, even if I didn't apply it. I was taken aback by his bluntness: "If you had a top-of-the-range sports car, you'd look after it and put premium fuel in it, right? You can replace that sports car, but you only have one body and you're putting any old shit in it."

Point taken, Doc.

I'd not really noticed the weight creep on during those few months. Even though I still hid my body, for the first time in many years I'd not been as pre-occupied with my weight. I'd stopped weighing myself in England.

We didn't have a full-length mirror in our new home, just a half one in the bathroom, so I never saw my body in its entirety. Without realising, I was also enjoying food guilt-free for the first time in years.

But the doctor's stark warning gave me a jolt. Heart disease ran in my family – Granda had been diagnosed with it – so I listened to the doctor's advice. The food-mall dinners went out the window and lean meats and healthy salads replaced them. Chocolate became a once-a-week treat rather than a daily compulsion and I began walking the two miles to work every day instead of driving. Within six months I lost all the weight I had gained but more importantly, my cholesterol returned to within a healthy range.

LOSS

JULY 1999

He manoeuvres the probe around inside me, his hand pushing down on my belly. The prodding hurts and I'm scared. The doctor has sent me to the hospital as my bloods show my hormone levels are dropping. This *shouldn't* be happening. I'm twelve weeks, four days' pregnant.

"I'm afraid there's no heartbeat. Your body isn't letting it go naturally, so you'll need to be booked in for surgery to remove it. Nurse, can you make the arrangements please" The doctor pulls the cold probe slowly out of my body. A condom and lube cover the instrument.

"But ... but I don't understand. I saw my baby's heartbeat on the scan last week, what happened?" I whisper weakly. I can barely speak, the lump in my throat is stopping me.

"It happens sometimes, the pregnancy wasn't viable – it's very common. Don't worry, once the surgery is done, you can try again in a few months," he advises matter-of-factly as he snaps his plastic examination gloves off, casting them in the bin, before getting up and leaving the room.

On to the next one.

I look at the nurse, stricken. I see the look in her eyes, I didn't imagine it. She doesn't approve of the way he just treated me, so coldly.

"Is that it? Why did he have to say it like that? This was my baby. It *is* my baby! I don't want to try for another one, I want this one, I want my baby back." I begin to sob.

The nurse touches my arm and soothes me. "I'm really so sorry, Emily."

I lie in bed that night, unable to sleep. My baby has died inside my body. My baby, the one who was due at Christmas, has died and my body isn't letting it go.

This is your fault. This is what you get for starving yourself. You've ruined your chances of having kids.

A couple of days later, I'm back home.

It's over.

I stand by the sideboard holding on, needing to steady myself. A hot, painful ball of grief is rising from my stomach and I can't stop it. A weight, heavy as stone, sits on my chest. I can't breathe but my mouth opens. A sound escapes I don't recognise, a wail like a wounded animal and I fall to my knees sobbing, my body convulsing with each painful wave.

I've lost my baby.

No, no, please make these feelings go away...

Not now. I'm not ready to feel this pain.

I want my mum.

In our late twenties, John and I decided to start a family. It took some time and one heartbreaking miscarriage before successfully getting pregnant for the second time. After the miscarriage, I was grateful to be pregnant again and welcomed the early telltale signs in my body for they signalled the pregnancy was developing normally: the ever-present mild nausea and slightly painful-to-the touch breasts.

By sixteen weeks though, I had a rounded belly. I didn't look pregnant yet, just a little heavy round the middle. I could just about see my belly in the bathroom mirror. *Will people think I'm just fat?* I wondered.

I dragged a dining chair to the bathroom and got up onto it carefully. Now all I could see was my belly. My heavy middle. To the front view, my waist had disappeared, to the side my belly stuck out.

It was a difficult phase in the pregnancy for me. I was so happy to be pregnant again and relieved to have passed twelve weeks, but I wanted to *look* pregnant. I didn't want to just look heavy; I wanted it to be visible and instantly recognisable.

As the pregnancy progressed, my body changed shape massively and this time, I welcomed it. I remember looking at the weight card that the midwife would fill in on each visit after she'd weighed me. Staying within normal weight-gain limits pleased me. I had worked hard to improve my health since my doctor's warning but more importantly to me, to lose weight. I was anxious not to put it all back on. I gained an average amount of weight during my pregnancy. It was one of the only times in my life that I was *almost* at peace with pronounced weight gain. Pregnancy legitimised it for me.

Thomas was born a full two weeks overdue and had to be induced. His birth was long and complex and I ended up staying in hospital for a week afterwards. The midwife had weighed me before I was discharged to gauge an antibiotics dose and had she not been there in the room, I would have punched the air in delight at my lighter-than-expected weight. At a time I should have been in a baby bubble of love, I was more in love with a post-birth weigh in. Losing weight certainly should not have been my first concern, but sadly it was. I had also gained new breasts the size of watermelons. Finally, I had a body shape that made me happy, even if I suffered a hard labour and engorged leaking breasts.

"Honey, I've got something to tell you..." Dad whispers. He begins to cry.

In June 2001, I returned home from hospital to discover my dad was terminally ill with cancer. He had been diagnosed when I was eight months pregnant and had his kidney removed. We both believed that he would recover. So did his oncologist. Sadly, that was not the case and the cancer had already spread to his spine.

I went into complete denial and pretended to myself, and him, that he would recover. I couldn't face the truth.

"No ... no. We will find a way. They must have it wrong. We will get a second opinion," I insisted, as my dad sat there holding his new-born grandson, crying. I was twenty-eight years old – too young to be preparing to bury a parent. I was raw and emotional already coping with my first-born and refused to allow the momentous tidal waves of pain to surface that would force me to face my dad's impending death.

The following weeks became a blur of sleepless nights, cracked nipples and leaking milk everywhere. I couldn't shake the overwhelming exhaustion I felt. My mind didn't have room to cope with my dad's cancer as well.

Four weeks after Thomas' birth I was back in hospital with an infection. Part of my placenta was retained after his birth. Thomas and I were admitted to hospital together so I could continue to feed him whilst I recovered from surgery to remove it. I remember welcoming the general anaesthetic that day – a heavy, cold numbness travelling up my arm, filling my body and sending me far away to sleep. *Someone else can take over and deal with all this for me,* I said to myself.

As I recovered from the surgery and tried to settle into new motherhood, dieting never entered my thoughts. Something had changed. For the first time since my childhood years, I viewed food as a source of fuel, this time to help my body breastfeed. I ate healthily and regularly, trying to keep up with my newfound ravenous appetite. Perhaps a maternal, primal instinct had kicked in. I had this baby who relied on me to feed him. I was in awe of him and of my body being able to sustain him.

I was also attending a mother's group and regular check-ups with the baby nurse and breast-feeding were encouraged. The focus shifted to Thomas's weight gain, not my weight loss. For some reason, my baby's weight gain became my new obsession, but I wasn't alone in that. Many of the new mums felt the same. Our babies' weight was recorded weekly and charted on a graph. We were constantly reminded by the health nurse that steady weight gain was one of the signs our babies were healthy and feeding well.

I was consumed with surviving new motherhood. Despite the baby books I'd read and the meticulous planning, nothing truly prepared me for my first child. Holding a fragile human being who was entirely dependent on me for his existence was overwhelming at times. That and the endless washing of vomit-covered clothes, nappy changes and feeding round the clock. The last thing I focused on was my body shape.

Life with a new baby was like an intensive boot camp; I just survived one gruelling exercise after another with naps in between during the first few months. And while I was dealing with the new-baby bedlam, John took over caring for my dad – he drove him to every oncologist appointment and treatment sessions. It was a relief to relinquish that role for a while.

Another interesting shift took place during the early months as I became a round-the-clock human dairy farm for Thomas. My body felt different, it was no longer a sexual object for John. My breasts became completely de-sexualised. They were purely for making milk and nurturing Thomas. They were leaky and lumpy and I stuffed my huge bras with cabbage leaves to soothe my cracked nipples whilst rubbing nappy cream on them to get through the painful weeks.

There was no room for or urge for sex. I was scared to try. Thomas had become stuck in the birth canal; the obstetrician had urged me to have a caesarean when forceps had failed to dislodge him. I pleaded with her to keep trying to deliver him vaginally – who knows why – but the next thing I remember, I'd been cut open with a scalpel and the obstetrician was inside my body, pulling my son out with a ventouse vacuum.

The aftermath was brutal and despite the countless stitches, the wound wouldn't heal up. The slightest attempt at intercourse tore me open once again. This went on for fourteen months until painful reconstruction surgery finally corrected it.

I guess for some women, 'getting back in the saddle' is part of reclaiming themselves as a partner, as a woman, and proving that their genitals still function sexually after birthing a whole human being out of them. I wished I had been one of those women, but the last thing on my mind at the time was intimacy.

For one thing, I didn't see myself as a woman anymore. I didn't see myself at all. I never looked in the mirror in the bathroom. The only view I ever had was looking down at my breasts as I fed Thomas. I saw myself as just a mother. A nurturer. And my dad's full-time carer.

When Thomas was five months old, I couldn't keep up with his food demands and was under increasing stress from my dad's diagnosis. Dad was terrified of dying and reverted to a childlike state at times. He needed me to comfort and reassure him – our roles had reversed.

The baby nurse encouraged me to continue breastfeeding, more often to stimulate more milk, but my nipples were sore, I had a cranky, hungry baby and a dying dad whose needs were growing. The formula bottles came out and I breathed again, in between bouts of immense guilt and feelings of maternal failure.

In May 2003, when Thomas was twenty months old, my dad lost the use of his legs. A tumour had grown around his spinal cord, paralysing him fully. I could no longer keep up with his daily care needs. I was washing and feeding him, and changing his bedding in between the nurses winching him up to change his adult nappies. It was desperately sad. Dad had lost his dignity and resented his illness. He also resented me waiting on him hand and foot too, but he feared dying and was often angry and sad, so he clung to me for comfort. I was faced with the difficult decision to place him in a hospice against his wishes, but his needs were greater than I could meet at home.

I was called to a meeting at the hospice to discuss Dad's resuscitation instructions not long after he moved in. His prognosis was six to nine months, maybe twelve at most, but it was a formality of his admission. I was thirty-one years old. It felt so wrong – I didn't want to play god. I didn't want the burden of choosing if he should live or die with this disease. I hadn't even accepted he was dying – despite him living in a hospice – and I couldn't bring myself to ask Dad what he wanted, for that would mean accepting it was real. So I left the meeting and said I would ask my family back in England for their advice. But I didn't. I avoided it once again.

A couple of months later, I had a call at work from the hospice. It was my dad. "*Emily... can you come to see me today. I'm scared. I'm dying...*" He barely managed a whisper.

"Of course I will come. Stop that now, you are not dying. I will be there at six tonight." I dismissed his fears, doing my best to reassure him.

That night, I collected Thomas from childcare after work and drove straight to the hospice. I wanted my dad to be pleased to see his grandchild, but he was in pain and instead he found the antics of a tired, whingeing toddler strapped in a pushchair irritating.

The doctor passed me in the carpark as I went in.

"My dad called me at work – how is he? He said he can't breathe and he's dying," I quizzed, stopping the doctor in his stride.

"He's doing ok, we have made him comfortable and I have given him an injection – he should be feeling much better in the morning," he reassured, before heading to his car.

Comforted, I headed in and sat with my dad. His breath was a little laboured and for the first time, I saw an old, sick man. It was as if the life had left his face. I stayed for an hour or so but by that stage Thomas was hungry and tired and arching his back in his pushchair, threatening to tip it over.

"Stop him crying, Emily, please," my dad wailed, the noise clearly agitating him further.

"I can't. He's tired and hungry. I will take him home and come back first thing in the morning, I promise," I soothed as I stood up, preparing to leave.

My dad grabbed my wrist firmly, stopping me from moving. "Don't leave me, Emily. Please don't leave me," he pleaded.

I was torn in two. Thomas was on one side crying, my dad on the other, begging me to stay. "I must go, I'm so sorry. I promise I will come back tomorrow."

I leant in and hugged him goodbye before turning the pushchair around and wheeling Thomas and his noisy racket away. It was a forty-minute drive home. Thomas fell asleep and I drove in autopilot, the peace allowing my mind to finally open to the reality that my dad wouldn't survive this illness.

Once I put Thomas to bed, I headed to bed, exhausted. I lay

in bed unable to sleep for hours, my mind racing over everything I'd never said to my dad; over everything I *should* have said.

"Are you awake...?" I prodded John awake. It was almost 1am but I needed someone to listen to me.

"Yes ... what is it? What is it, Emily?" John answered, half-asleep.

"I'm going to take the day off work tomorrow. I'm going in to spend the day with my dad. I'm going to tell him I'm sorry... I'm going to..." I trailed off into silence, the lump in my throat preventing me from continuing. I'd finally accepted my dad was dying.

"I'm going to tell him I love him ... and I'm going to call him 'Dad'. I need to say it."

I started to weep. The unspoken void between us needed healing before it was too late.

John pulled me closer, wrapping his arm around my shoulders, pulling my head to lay on his chest. As he held me, I drifted off to sleep knowing what needed to be done.

Just after 3am the phone rang, waking Thomas up. I went to the hallway to pick it up, wondering who would be calling at that time. Occasionally Ryan would get the time difference wrong and call in the middle of the night, a little worse for wear after a night out on the drink.

"Hello?"

"Hello, is that Emily?" a gentle voice enquired.

"Yes, that's me. Who is this?" I quizzed, slightly alarmed. It wasn't Ryan.

"My name is Sarah and I'm a nurse at the Orchard Hospice. I'm very sorry to tell you that your father passed away about half an hour ago."

"No...no. *No*," I snapped in disbelief.

It wasn't true and maybe if I said no enough times, just maybe it would change.

"I'm really sorry. Would you like to come and spend some time with your dad before the undertaker comes?"

"Ok..." I whispered and hung the phone up.

I stood there completely numb, anchored to the spot, unable to move or feel or process anything.

John appeared behind me and quietly placed his arms around me, snapping me back into a sharp awareness of my body.

"He's gone. I'm going to see him," I said blankly.

There were no tears, not yet, because there was nothing, no emotion, just emptiness and disbelief.

John called me a taxi and by 5am I was walking through the doors of the hospice I'd left the night before. I was greeted by two nurses.

"Your father passed away very quickly." One nurse smiled and rubbed my arm soothingly. "He didn't feel any pain."

She turned and headed towards the phone that was ringing on the reception desk.

"Did he know he was dying?" I said to the other nurse. I needed to know. I wanted his death to have been easy on him.

"Ah actually, he was very scared."

She tilted her head and gave me a look of sympathy, as if this statement should somehow comfort me. I could tell that English was her second language and perhaps her words had become lost in translation.

"What... *What...??* Why would you tell me that?" I shouted back, angry at her clumsy revelation.

The other nurse heard the commotion and returned and led me to a family room. It was minimally decorated in muted blue tones with a lonely sofa and a sad-looking lily wilting on the windowsill of the opaque window.

And then the inevitable rush happened – a tidal wave of shock and an unhealed relationship that had been firmly held back behind a dam of denial for so long, broke. I sobbed, my body convulsing in waves of grief. "Why... Why... *Why*?" I wailed in between sobs.

The nurse sat me down and passed me tissues from the box – she was the only thing of any warmth in the sterile room.

"But I spoke to the doctor last night, he told me he was fine. He said he would feel better today. Why... Why did he die? What happened?" I pleaded for answers.

'Your father was having difficulty breathing. He was very sick and I'm afraid we couldn't save him," she soothed.

My dad had given up and his body had given in. He'd known he was dying the day before, yet I hadn't listened to him and I had left him to die alone and scared. My emotions were starting to seep back into my body and I began shaking. The nurse remained with me until I settled.

"I'm going to leave you and when you are ready to see your father, come and get me and I will take you in," she said, rubbing my forearm gently.

I sat silently in stillness, numb. I had pushed my dad's illness and impending death away for two years. I hadn't made my peace with him and it was my fault he had died alone and scared in a hospice. A pain twisted in my stomach, steely knives of guilt and grief turning over the flesh.

After three hours sitting in the family room avoiding the inevitable, the nurse reappeared. "Would you like to come and see your father? I'm sorry to rush you, but the undertakers will be arriving at 11am to take him away."

I had no idea what to expect. I'd never seen a dead body before. I didn't know how I should feel.

"Ok," I whispered, unconvinced I could face what I needed to do.

The nurse led me to my dad's room and opened the door,

gesturing me to follow her. He was lying on a bed; a white sheet covering his body completely.

I fled the room, unable to face him like that, a lifeless body under a sheet heading for the mortuary.

"Can you take the sheet off his face, please? I can't... I just can't do it." I looked at the nurse with fear-filled eyes.

"Of course I can." She smiled kindly before disappearing and returning a moment later.

"I will leave you alone now. Take your time, okay?" she offered gently, leaving me standing in front of the heavy wooden door.

When I went back into the room, the white sheet had been folded down neatly across my dad's chest, his hands placed together as if in prayer. His pale fingers appearing to be holding a dark red rose in an attempt to present him in a peaceful way, but the staging unnerved me.

I stood staring, not knowing how to feel or what to say. Pain flooded my body physically, deep in the pit of my stomach, rising and constricting my chest – a pain I'd only felt once before after losing my baby. The tears fell once more.

I walked to my dad's side. He looked peaceful and much younger, as if all the cancer and pain that had recently aged him had drained from his face. At fifty-nine, he was still young and handsome, with just a few salt-and-pepper greys dusting the curls on his temples. I waited for him to move or speak, but he didn't. I reached out and touched his hand and quickly pulled away.

It was cold. Empty and lifeless.

"Why... Why did you have to die now?" I cried at him, half-expecting him to wake up and answer me, but he didn't.

"Bye... Da..." I stopped myself. Even in death, I couldn't bring myself to say it.

"I love you. I've always loved you..." I whispered and I fled the room, unable to look back.

The following few days passed in a timeless blur and I slipped into a numb autopilot state preparing for my dad's funeral. I stopped eating. Pain replaced hunger. I couldn't put food in my mouth, the thought of it sickened me. I was feasting on guilt and regret instead. *I didn't get to say goodbye. I didn't get to tell him I'm sorry*, I told myself over and over.

I remember lying in bed listening to people pass my bedroom window, laughing and joking and carrying on with life. I resented their joy and normality. How could they be happy?

Sitting alone in the front pew of the funeral service was the loneliest I'd ever felt. Neither my mum nor Ryan could access the funds needed to get to Australia at such short notice. This was my burden alone and deep inside, I felt I owed my dad this. I'd let him down and he had died alone because of me – giving him a decent send-off was the least I could do.

John was carrying my dad's coffin, along with several of my dad's friends. I was aware of the crowd that had gathered behind me but didn't dare turn around to acknowledge anyone in case I lost my composure. I was determined to be the dutiful daughter, to give him a funeral he would have been proud of and not collapse in the puddle of tears I knew was inevitable if someone should offer me comfort.

The modern crematorium housed a couple of hundred people and my dad's passing had filled it full. This quiet unassuming man had affected many lives throughout his life in Australia and they had come to his final gig to send him off in style. His favourite guitar sat propped up against his coffin with two cans of his favourite beer placed on top: a couple of drinks for the long road home.

One by one, people filed up and said their silent goodbyes: women, men, musicians, rockers, roadies, bartenders and a handful of my friends too.

Finally, the coffin began to lower and its descent was the slowest, most painful final realisation that my dad was gone. I turned to face the crowd behind me – one I'd been avoiding for half an hour – and thanked them all, one by one, as they filed out and left the crematorium.

The wake was a celebration of his life, just as he would have wanted it to be – a casual party in a garden overlooking the Indian Ocean until long after the sun had set with guitars, music and beer. My dad would have enjoyed his final gig.

After the party was over, I allowed the tears to fall. After a funeral, we are expected to move along with life, as if the service marks the end of our pain. But it's only a part of loss – a stage of grief, the beginning, not the end and I couldn't cope with the pain I felt. It was so heavy, it felt like a physical stone weighted in the pit of my stomach. I couldn't welcome the grief surfacing to heal it, I was scared to feel that pain and overwhelmed with guilt, so instead, I buried it deeply and began a new diet.

A NEW LIFE

JULY 2004

I DEVELOPED COMPLICATIONS FROM THOMAS'S BIRTH AND the subsequent surgeries had left me infertile in my late twenties. John and I had spent a year on the fertility treatment rollercoaster throughout the end of my dad's life. The medications made me feel nauseous, so I ate sparingly to hold off the nausea. Life was hectic. Thomas was toddling by then and I was back working for the Australian government part-time.

Within three months of my father's death, Jack was conceived through fertility treatment and my focus shifted from my low-carb diet and rather pleasing eight-pound weight loss to my new pregnancy.

My third pregnancy was different to Thomas' and my body felt extremely uncomfortable the second time round. Everything ached and I didn't enjoy the changes. Angry red stretch marks ran across my breasts and my legs and ankles were swollen. It was a fraught pregnancy.

After complications and threat of miscarriage at seventeen weeks, the next few months revolved around hospital visits, blood tests and scans. By six months, I felt like I was nestling a bowling ball on my cervix, convinced the baby would fall out at any moment. At thirty-four weeks, he arrived early and unannounced by emergency caesarean due to his breach position.

A caesarean hadn't been in my plan. I'd planned a water birth with essential oils in diffusers and relaxing music; a natural birth, something less fraught than Thomas' birth. I had a plan all ready and drawn up and that vanished in the scrambled speed of an emergency c-section six weeks early.

I know some women may say a caesarean is an easy option, but for me it really wasn't. I kept fainting after the birth every time I stood up. I developed an infection in my wound that saw me on strong antibiotics for three weeks. I was in pain and crying, struggling to hold and feed my premature baby.

The recovery was slow and painful; after all, they are slicing through several layers of your abdomen – it's major surgery. My body didn't bounce back as quickly this time. The scar was large and uneven, like a lopsided smile. It healed slowly and eventually thickened to a toughened scar. The stitches had pulled me in tightly over the pubic bone, like a human girdle, but my twice-stretched belly sat above it, hanging over the scar uncomfortably; unattractively to me. I should have worn this as a miracle medal, proof of life. But I didn't.

As the dust settled on my grief and I adjusted to two young sons, life changed for me. I struggled to lose the baby weight from Jack. I was swept up in running after two young children and the focus entirely switched to them and their needs. I stopped paying my marriage attention. Unconsciously, I pushed John away. It was as if there wasn't any room for him, or us, or even me. My role as a mother consumed me. I'd lost one baby and my father – that overwhelming fear of losing another loved one made me hold on very tightly to my sons.

I was still conscious about my weight but between running after two kids, a husband and working a part-time job during the heat of Australian summers, my weight stayed constant, albeit higher than I wanted.

A couple of years after my dad's death, I began to check the calorific value of food once again and would study the number of kilocalories on food packaging in the supermarket. If the calories were over the 200-calorie mark, it entered my self-declared 'danger zone' and even then, after all those years, I still labelled certain foods as sinful or 'naughty'. The forbidden foods were always the tastiest ones too: crisps, chips, chocolate, cake, cheese, pastry, pizza...

I had pigeonholed food as 'good' or 'bad' many years before, labels that had never really left me and sat nicely with my belief that being slimmer meant being happier. It was an attitude reinforced by the diet culture and shocking heroin chic of the 1990s – one that glorified painfully thin catwalk models. Carbs and sugar were considered bad in my books and the media. I avoided the 'bad' stuff like the plague most of the time. But on rare occasions, I allowed myself to eat them.

The trouble was, once I started, it was hard to stop.

The marble cake is sitting on the kitchen bench. It's still warm, just out of the oven. I made it myself. It's Mum's recipe. I've licked the bowl clean – and the spoon. I ate a couple of tablespoons of the raw cake batter from the tin too, before it went in.

Two tablespoons aren't enough really. I want more.

I love that taste. The gritty sweet sugar coated in whipped butter, smooth and silky like an extra-thick milkshake ... with raw egg and flour. But it doesn't matter. Nobody saw.

Now that it's baked, I pick at the edges, the crunchier, well-baked bits. I love those too. And the layer of cake bubbles that cover the top. I peel them off and eat them all. But what a mess

I've made of this cake now! I'll dust it with icing sugar and the kids won't know.

I cut into the cake – the knife glides right through. It's too warm really but I can't wait. I can't help myself.

One big slice down. Now two. A third of the cake has gone.

I feel a bit sick now.

Thomas runs in from the garden. "Mummy, is the cake ready?"

"Yes, love. Do you want some?"

What have I done?

That's it! You can't have anything else to eat today, Emily.

There was so much guilt attached to eating those foods I usually avoided. Overwhelming, suffocating, punishing guilt for eating cake, especially when I couldn't seem to control my portions. I'd not committed any real crimes, yet eating those foods filled me with immense guilt every time.

Despite the shame and my body-weight concerns, I could be a sneaky carb-eater back then too. I found it difficult to moderate my portions when I allowed myself to eat them – a common response to deprivation of a particular food group. Put me in front of a buffet at a party and I'd be the one looking from side to side, checking the coast was clear, before stuffing one mini pizza in my mouth as fast as I could and placing one on my plate. I did this with all the self-labelled 'naughty' foods along the buffet. Two for one: one for my mouth and one for my plate. It was as if once I started, I couldn't satiate the carb-craving enough. I had to get my fill whilst I could. I had to keep going until I felt uncomfortably full, or sick, or if I thought someone had rumbled my behaviour.

I once went to a friend's charity afternoon tea and there was the most incredible spread of sweet treats. The host's daughter was a pastry chef. I did one round of the table with my paper plate piled up, but the sugar rush of the deliciously gooey triple chocolate brownies triggered that 'must have more' feeling.

I ended up having six, amongst shortcakes, cupcakes and fresh jam tarts. Forget the sandwiches or sausage rolls, this was all about sugar. I watched the other ladies chatting and delicately taking an occasional bite of a cupcake and it made me very conscious of the amount I could consume, which made the behaviour even more secretive. I remember the host passing comment to her daughter about the brownies being popular and secretly cringeing, hoping no one had noticed that their swift disappearance was mostly down to me.

If I was going to a wedding, my mind was always preempting what might be served at the wedding breakfast or evening buffet rather than the nuptials themselves. I was obsessed with food. The taste, the texture, the momentary pleasure but most of all, the calories. I began flipping between depriving and gorging myself quite regularly.

At thirty-four, I found my periods were becoming more irregular. My cycle was unpredictable and I never felt as if my body had fully recovered from either of my sons' pregnancies and the four surgeries it had taken to give them life. If my period was late, I panicked. Not mildly either, but with an overwhelming irrational fear of pregnancy. Not that there was much chance of it happening unless it was a Holy Immaculate Conception – sex was a distant memory.

But mentally, there was no way I felt able to cope with pregnancy again, neither physically nor emotionally. My doctor referred me back to my gynaecologist – the same specialist who ran the fertility clinic who had successfully enabled Jack's pregnancy and repaired the damage from Thomas's birth through several subsequent surgeries.

He checked my hormone levels and they showed I had the oestrogen levels of a pre-menopausal woman. I wasn't surprised – my mum had gone through an early menopause in her forties. Despite my potential perimenopausal hormones and lack of any sex life, the risk of pregnancy for me was far too great and not one I was prepared to take a gamble on, so I chose a more drastic contraception option – permanent sterilisation. It was my body and I wanted the choice – a way to control something and end my irrational fear for good. A few months later, I went into hospital and had my fallopian tubes clamped. It was a forced end to my reproductive years by choice and something so at odds from the woman who had endured so much to conceive and carry life just a few years earlier.

Although life was keeping me busy, by my mid-thirties I was a little numb inside. I didn't recognise it then and just kept adding things to my calendar to keep me occupied. I needed something that helped the emptiness of my thoughts, so I distracted myself with food once again. Not eating it ... but cooking it.

FOOD IS LOVE

2007

Without a great deal of consideration, I quit the boring-but-safe government job at the local benefits office I had been in for ten years. It had worn me down and I never felt up to standard since returning part-time after the birth of Jack. Motherhood felt like a barrier to progressing up the corporate ranks – maybe that was in my own mind through lack of confidence and shifting priorities as a mother, but I never felt I would be able to climb any further on the government ladder. I wasn't even sure I wanted to. It wasn't that I didn't want to work, it was just I had no fire left for that job. Day after day spent sitting in the benefits office being verbally abused by people was just part of the territory.

John panicked – I'd never been unemployed and my decision to resign from the financial safety of a government job caught him off-guard. He needn't have worried – it was 2007 and work was plentiful in Western Australia.

Within a week I took a part-time job working in a café as a kitchen assistant. Unbeknown to me, they wanted a second-in-charge chef to cover the Head Chef on his days off. I was in way over my head and out of my gastronomical depth. I lasted six weeks, unable to manage the demands of a hot kitchen, a busy menu and fraught chef, with no more experience than that of cooking for my husband and kids. But the stint around food whet my appetite (pardon the pun) and I soon landed a job as an assistant manager in a new Indian restaurant opening in a shopping-mall food court in Perth. The chef, Raju, was a quiet young man in his early twenties from South India. He had recently arrived in Australia and was keen to impress his new bosses. India's colourful culture and spirituality had interested me for years, so there was something so enriching working alongside Raju. Listening to his stories of his home in Kerala settled my desire to go there, but it was never going to happen: John's only interest in India was its cricket score.

Raju called me his Indian sister and I took him under my wing, caring for him. I was in my element in my new role, watching the gentle-mannered chef prepare his Indian delights from scratch. Raju would explain the importance of each ingredient as he taught me the recipes. I never tired of the smells of the fresh ginger, garlic, spices and onions frying.

Most days, when no one was watching, I'd steal a fresh garlic naan bread from the neat rows that were laid out under the hot lights. They were my favourite. The glistening garlic butter was too tempting to resist. I'd stash it under the counter along with a pot of the curry sauce of the day, usually the butter chicken, swimming in rich ghee. I'd choose my moment and dip a crudely torn chunk of naan in the sauce and pop it in my mouth without anyone noticing. Often it was on a pretend bend-down to get napkins or replenish cutlery. There was pleasure both in my mouth and in the secrecy of the manoeuvre.

I'd stand at the helm of this food fishbowl observing people sitting in the food court chatting and enjoying their lunch and feel immense satisfaction when they would return to thank the chef for their Indian feast. It was very different from the benefits office. Nobody ever shouted at me here.

At the end of every shift, after we'd washed up and cleaned down, the other vendors would swap leftovers and I would head home at night with everything from Mexican burritos, Italian pastas, muffins and sushi and everything in between, much to my kids' delight.

This food business was alright after all. People loved to eat and I loved to please people, so what better way to please people than through food?

Cushions are scattered across the floor: woven gold thread, with pink and orange designs. A large, stitched rug covers the wooden floor. Silver stars hang above our heads. Tea lights everywhere gently glow, casting soft light upon twenty or so faces and Indian music is quietly playing behind a room full of conversation.

In the middle of the floor are four large crates covered in colourful saris – they are makeshift tablecloths but nobody notices. The guests sit on the floor in anticipation. The smells from the kitchen leave them salivating.

I deliver a large tray and lay it before them – eight silver bowls containing a lamb rogan josh, its rich gravy smothering the meat, tender from days of marinating; chicken korma bathed in a creamy orange sauce and sweetly aromatic; pilau rice, spiced with fragrant cardamon and star anise; a spicy jalfrezi, its red and green peppers adding flashes of colour; onion bhajis and vegetable samosas. A pile of freshly fried papadums are stacked in a golden tower served alongside pickles and chutneys. It is an Indian feast. I stand back watching and bask in the noises of appreciation as my guests eat the food that has taken me three days to make.

I used the skills Raju taught me and began to throw Indian dinner parties cooking from scratch, sometimes preparing gastronomical feasts for days beforehand. If I was never going to go to India, I would bring the country to me.

I turned my dining room into a magical Indian oasis, draping rich golden-threaded fabric from the ceiling in great swathes and sewing little glittering stars with invisible cotton into the fabric so that they danced magically in the candlelight. The guests would sit on cushions on the floor, mingling and marvelling at the dining extravaganza experience I gave them. I was in my element, but I rarely permitted myself to eat the food I made.

I became obsessed with food presentation long before Instagram was a thing and when I dished up my culinary delights, I'd stand back and watch my guests' faces light up at the edible art on the plate in front of them. I'd found a way to express myself through art *and* please people. But I had also found a way to derive pleasure vicariously through watching others eat. I felt excited – almost euphoric – watching their sensory reactions to food. They gave me pleasure without even knowing and kept all the calories away from me.

As the popularity of the dinner parties grew, a friend suggested I sell my curries so I decided to set up my own business from home. Twice a week, I'd deliver fresh curries to order. And as that grew, I branched into catering for John's football team and their families twice a month.

Everything was made from scratch, even pastry and bread. I would spend the entire weekend prepping, baking, cooking and loved every moment. I enjoyed my own company and would get lost in the food preparation. John was proud of me and was happy to have a wife who fed his teammates, so he didn't object.

On Sunday afternoons, as the footballers were showering in a foggy changing room filled with menthol rub, I'd be delivering vast feasts ready to feed up the players and their families. Standing on the side-lines of the club room, I'd watch in quiet delight as they devoured my creations and fuss about them, refilling their plates and cleaning up afterwards, often refusing help. I enjoyed the exclusive recognition they gave me as the team cook. Food made me happy. Feeding people made me happier. Food was my new language of love.

"Just take some then!"

John angrily dropped his cutlery on the table in protest, pushing his plate towards me. I'd been eyeing up his golden wedges across the restaurant table. My garden salad felt wholesome but uninteresting and his fried potatoes looked so tempting. I couldn't order myself a portion: that would break the latest diet. But I could look at his, I could pine for them without saying a word and I often did and it irritated John. He was one of six kids and food was scarce growing up. Nothing was ever spare on his plate.

I leant across and took one from his plate and he pulled it back and carried on eating his meal. I bit down on the potato wedge. The gloriously salty, warm, golden oily potato wedge melted in my mouth.

Wait, that's about sixty-two calories, I thought. *How much fat was in that potato wedge? Maybe it wasn't worth irritating John for.*

I returned to my salad, disgusted with myself for caving in.

And now John was angry at me too. John had volunteered his food to me on that occasion, unwillingly, but what he didn't know and neither did my children, was that I regularly stole food from their plates before serving it to them. Potatoes, pasta, crisps, pastry, bread – whatever I usually forbid myself was stolen in small quantities. It wasn't enough that they would notice, but enough to satiate the taste for me without ruining the latest diet I was on.

Stealing food was nothing new: I had stolen food before, mostly chocolate as a child: from the pantry, from presents under the Christmas tree, Ryan's Easter eggs from his bedroom. What child doesn't do that? But those behaviours had carried on throughout my life. I'd delight in the scraps my children left on their plates. I could eat them all, and I did – and not just my children's. I welcomed cleaning up after my son's birthday parties, for I was guaranteed a buffet of half-eaten fairy cakes or chocolate crackles destined for the bin. They mostly went in a human bin: me.

I scraped the remnants off people's plates in restaurants during my waitressing days, silently tutting at the patrons for wasting perfectly good chips and crispy fish batter – the best bit – or half-eaten naan breads. More than once, I considered eating their scraps off the plates. Sometimes I did: a sneaky chip here and there in the middle of a pile. *No sign of saliva or spat out food*, I'd reason.

What kind of person steals food from other people's plates? A stranger's plate?

Me.

CRACKS

2008

I'M STANDING IN FRONT OF THE DRESSING-TABLE MIRROR IN my bedroom. John's in the swimming pool with the boys. My hair is a short bob now. Blonde highlights and a haircut were meant to change the way I feel but they don't, not really.

My curls are gone now – ironed down straight every day.

I'm just a wife and a mum.

I look at my face, I see new lines and wrinkles. Just a few, but it's already begun.

I turn to the side. I assess my profile.

These breasts are fuller.

My hand cups my belly, a round belly, obvious to anyone. Ugly to some.

I turn to the front. My hips are wider.

I look at my eyes, the sparkle has gone.

I look at my face, it's round like the moon.

Moon-face mum.

As I moved through my mid-thirties, I became increasingly shut off from my feelings and emotions. I felt numb a lot of the time and couldn't understand my apathy. I *should* have been happy. On the surface, I had a husband who adored me, two healthy sons and the stereotypical perfect family life in a beautiful home on the sunny shores of Australia. But behind the scenes, I was a woman with undiagnosed depression and that heavy black cloud wrapped itself around my life and blocked out my sun. Depression wasn't spoken of back then. I never understood *why* I felt so numb.

I had no physical connection to John since having my children. My body had changed: filled out, sagged, wrinkled a little. I hated my bigger body. I didn't want to look at it. I didn't want him to see it, to touch it. I didn't deserve pleasure and I didn't take it.

John didn't care that my body had changed in all those years spent together – so had his. He loved *me*, Emily. I was the mother of his children and his love ran so deeply for me. But I was lost and deeply depressed, I couldn't feel anything emotionally and I pushed him away. His attempts at affection were mostly rebutted. Instead, I hugged my children and experienced that necessary connection and warmth through my young sons' dependence on me.

I continued to fill a gnawing emptiness I didn't understand with dinner parties, catering and themed children's parties for my sons, much to the delight of Thomas and Jack and their friends. My sons had friends over most nights and the noise of the neighbours' kids splashing in the pool cut through the silence I dreaded. Entertaining others seemed to be my only real source of pleasure.

I continued to wander for another year through life like a Stepford wife, complete with perfectly manicured front lawn in front of the shiny car in a neat garage. It was my idyllic home in the sunshine containing two happy healthy kids and a husband who adored me. But it wasn't quite enough.

I always seemed caught in an endless loop of '*If I can just get...*' thoughts. If I could just get this new sofa, or paint the family room, or just get that *thing*, I will reach that happy place, that sweet spot where everything will feel better, where I will just feel something, other than the void inside.

I'd worked hard since the age of fifteen and finally by my late thirties had found financial stability and a home in the sun for my young, healthy family. But no matter how many candles and cushions we bought or how many coats of paint we put on the walls, I couldn't find the sweet spot of happiness.

I'd become very isolated in Perth. Dad had been dead several years and I had no other family there. One by one, my grandparents died back in the UK and Ireland. I'd lost an uncle and a young cousin and their deaths forced me to face my own mortality for the first time. I missed my mum. I suddenly felt lonely in that big house in the most isolated place in the world. Maybe going back home to England would make things feel better?

John had sensed my mood dipping and my disconnection from him. I must have hurt him with my constant pushbacks yet he continued in his attempts to please me. It was that deep love he held for me that enabled me to convince John into selling our home and packing up our entire life for a completely different one back home in the UK. It was financially suicidal as the UK was in a recession in 2010 and we had no job prospects, but I convinced him nevertheless and within six months we were back in the UK, in temporary accommodation and unemployed.

The pressures of such a big sea-change caused cracks in our

relationship of twenty-three years. Everything had changed for me. But the one thing that remained constant was my love of being around food.

I found a job in a restaurant and fell back into the role of the feeder, cooking sweet treats for the staff and watching their delight as they tucked in after their shifts. Every week it was something new: blueberry cheesecake, double-chocolate brownies, warm apple pies. These were soon discovered by the boss who tasked me with coming up with a dessert for the restaurant. Once again, food gave me a route to recognition and that attention made me feel like *someone* again. My dessert landed on the menu and word spread and soon I had a small dessert business, working from home and supplying local cafés and restaurants.

During that time, I was neither bingeing nor intentionally depriving myself of food – in fact, most of the time I forgot to eat, far too pre-occupied with food in a different capacity. I had slipped back into deriving pleasure from others eating it, but the accidental weight loss quietly delighted my inner troll. *You look so much better slimmer*, it said.

My waitressing job meant working with a much younger group of staff. They bounced off each other with a youthful exuberance I found myself drawn to. I really enjoyed waitressing. I'd fallen into something that allowed me to serve people and witness their pleasure in food. I no longer felt the same urges to consume it. In a strange way, watching others' pleasure from food filled that desire and I often found myself staring at people as they ate, smiling.

The job made me feel alive and I was feeding that newfound fire for life by spending time with the youthful staff. Their energy rubbed off on me. There were a couple of young lads in their early twenties who would joke with me flirtatiously and I reciprocated in harmless innocence, enjoying the feeling of these men admiring me. I'd never flirted. John was my first and only boyfriend. These men didn't see me as a mother or a wife, they saw me as Emily and I liked the way that made me feel.

After a Friday night out in a pub with my colleagues after our shift, I'd snuck in late and went straight to bed with a brooding John lying next to me in the dark. The next day he accused me of having an affair.

John wasn't too happy with my newfound enthusiasm for work or my young colleagues. It made his own insecurities surface. He saw his wife beginning to glow again and it wasn't because of him.

John's accusation tripped the love switch in me that had been faltering for the latter part of twenty-three years and within three weeks I found myself a single woman again.

DISCOVERING ME

JULY 2011

I'M STANDING IN FRONT OF MY NEW FULL-LENGTH MIRROR, naked. My eyes are closed. I'm too scared to look. I've not had a mirror like this for a long time, just bathroom mirrors or a dressing table one.

It's been many years since I've looked at my entire body in the flesh. No one else has seen it either, not even John. Since having the kids ten years ago, I have kept my body covered in bed, only removing my clothes for sex.

I hesitate at first, almost unable to look and I wince as I stand in front of the mirror, naked. I can't bear to look at my own skin but I have to.

I open my eyes and stare at my breasts, small and uneven, the left one slightly larger than the right. I long for neat pert nipples of a magazine model, yet all I see are the large areolas that I've always loathed. These breasts have fed and nurtured my sons for months and given me so many precious memories of those early morning feeds. But now, as a thirty-eight-year-old, single woman, all I can see are the physical consequences of those early months of maternal duty.

My eyes dart downwards to my stomach – a dot-to-dot

pattern of large moles; my back has even more, a parting gift from the Greek islands. They have stretched during my pregnancies and not returned. No tan was worth these skin souvenirs.

I slowly trace my fingers around the curve of my caesarean scar nestled above my pubic bone. It's long and uneven, the darker scar tissue from the post-op infection exaggerating the thickness. I've never examined it fully, ever. In parts it's still numb to touch, the nerves clearly damaged by surgery. My stomach sits above it, a small ledge of flesh. It overhangs the heavy scar.

I turn to the side. I want the truth – I need confirmation of my own repulsion.

It's a shame you didn't get a tummy tuck thrown in with the C-section.

Will anyone ever love me again?

DISCOVERING MEN

DECEMBER 2011

SINGLE LIFE BROUGHT WITH IT MANY FIRST-TIME experiences for me, including my first bikini wax at home, a belly-button piercing, underwear shopping for the first time ever – not your multipack, big-knicker kind of underwear that you mismatch with your comfiest bra, I went for sexy silk and lace lingerie that actually matched. I wanted to feel beautiful in my skin and found that underwear hid all the bits of my body I hated the most – just about. If I was ever going to share this body sexually again, I wanted to feel pretty and feminine.

But first, I needed to be slimmer. Out went the breakfasts and regular meals and bowls of soup and cereal and bananas replaced them. And as a result, my weight began to drop again.

Within a matter of months into singledom, I caught the eye of Andre, a younger French man, on a night out with some work friends. He was a friend of a friend and the spark was there from the beginning. Andre's skin was tanned and his hair, thick and lusciously curly and at 6' 4", he towered over me. He studied interior design at college and had an interest in fashion. His creativity fascinated me.

We began hanging out from time to time, just as friends, when my sons were with John. Sometimes we'd meet in a bar, or perhaps go out for dinner. Occasionally, Andre would indulge in his interest in fashion and would take us both clothes shopping.

"I think this one is good. You try for me?" Andre directed, holding up a beautiful long dress, iceberg-blue silk, after gently going through the clothing racks in a top-end store. "It matches your eyes, no?

"Okay, let me try it on." I smiled, disappearing into the changing cubicle. No man had ever dressed me before.

I pulled the dress on excitedly. Turning to the side, it did everything it needed to. It was loose-fitting and pretty. I sucked in my belly and it almost disappeared. I looked at my eyes. Andre was right, the dress matched them perfectly.

I tipped my head upside-down, fluffed up my curls and put on some lippy. *Make yourself look pretty for him*, I thought.

I pull back the curtain, shyly. "What do you think?"

"It's beautiful, Emily."

Andre was great at playing a girl's best friend – he *loved* to go clothes shopping. He knew what colours complimented my hair and what suited my skin tone. He chose the finest Italian silk dresses that covered my body elegantly with designer leather handbags and shoes to match. I bought him fine coffee afterwards and he bought me delicate French cakes.

These outings began as platonic dates but as we rode the train back home together, his large warm arms pressed against mine. I began to fantasise what it would be like to kiss him, and more.

One weekend, the boys were staying with John and I decided to treat myself to a spa package deal in a nearby hotel, another first for me. It was a Sunday night and the hotel was half-empty. As a therapist massaged my back, my mind wandered to my young friend ... and my new underwear. A delicious feeling danced in my belly, unfamiliar to me: the excitement of new desire.

After a swim – exactly thirty-five laps, enough to burn off the required number of calories – I went back to my room and showered before slipping into my new lace underwear. I looked in the mirror at myself, this time without hesitation or revulsion. It's incredible what a scrap of lace and silk can do to a woman's ego.

Perching on the side of the bed, legs crossed, posing elegantly, feeling like an underwear model in my head, I picked up my phone. *Should I text him?* I asked myself. *No, don't be ridiculous.*

I put the phone back down again and ordered room service still sitting in my underwear, not feeling brave enough to sit in the hotel restaurant alone. I couldn't face making polite conversation with a waiter or a coach load of pensioners, there for their annual winter holiday by the sea.

It felt decadent to order room service. It was only a bowl of vegetable soup with a side salad but I wasn't used to anyone catering for me. My soup felt even more special being served under a silver dome with a crisp, white napkin.

With the Dutch courage of a garden salad, I began a one-sided conversation with myself: *Come on, Emily, it won't hurt, it's just one night. You can do this!*

I picked up my phone and texted Andre quickly before I changed my mind: *"Hi, I'm staying at the Heatherfields Hotel if you're in town and want to meet up tonight for a drink x"*

That was as casual as I could make it sound. I didn't even drink, but it sounded good. It was my first text to a single man, ever.

My insides were doing somersaults as I paced the room to pass the time. On went the TV, then off again.

Throwing open the balcony doors, I stared out at the sea. The cold, grey English Channel whipped in white peaks in the squally December wind. It wasn't exactly *Casablanca*.

The bedside table vibrated with the buzz of my phone and my stomach flipped. There, the familiar banner alerting a text message and his name: *"Sure, which room are you in? Will be there about ten after work."*

No kisses?

We both knew he wasn't just coming for a drink. The last two months of friendly flirtation had been building to something.

I panicked. *Shit, what have I got myself into?!* I thought.

I'd been separated for six months from John yet it still felt like infidelity to even contemplate seeing another man after twenty-three years. The thing was, I was no longer John's; his wife, yes, but only on paper. I was single and this secret rendezvous was long overdue.

It was the longest two hours ever as I tried to distract myself by watching TV and painting my toenails. I saw images but didn't hear a thing, just my own inner monologue over why this wasn't such a good idea. At least I had some clothes on now, but the new underwear was still lying underneath them. I checked my side profile three times just to confirm if my belly was flat enough for Andre.

Andre arrived just after ten. He was smartly dressed and smelt of sensual cologne. He headed to the balcony and lit a cigarette, whilst opening a bottle of beer. Andre turned to me, offering me one, but I declined. The blustery wind blew his smoke away before it had time to linger around me.

And then it happened – Andre leant over and kissed me. I'd never kissed another man before. It intrigued me to experience another man's mouth, to feel his kiss and how it differed to John's; to taste a cigarette and beer from someone's tongue. It was more intriguing in its unfamiliarity than unpleasant.

Andre slowly unbuttoned my dress and I stood before him in my new lace underwear, feeling small and unsure rather than confident and brave. But the setting was perfect – a balcony, the waves in the background, soft lighting. This was my own movie set and I was the leading lady.

Andre stared at my body. "What's wrong? Why you look so scared?" He must have sensed my hesitation and fear.

"I'm nervous, Andre. I've never been with anyone other than my ex-husband." I looked down at my feet. *At least my nails look pretty*, I thought.

"And so? I haven't either, just one woman. It's life. It's okay, you have ... bits in all the right places," he attempted to reassure me.

I panicked. "What does that mean?!"

Andre shrugged without answering. It was a compliment of sorts but it was somewhat lost in translation.

Andre had only had one lover in his lifetime but it seemed that most of his sex education had been learnt through watching porn and he practiced those moves on me. In me. There was no tenderness.

Was this what it felt like to be with another man? Is this what life outside the familiarity of my marriage was really like?

After it was over, I lay in the darkness of the room I'd paid for, in the bed I had shared with someone else for the first time, listening to a different man snore and I wept.

The next morning was uncomfortable. Somethings are best left unspoken, but I yearned for some sort of recognition. Sharing my body in such an intimate way at my stage of life felt like it should have been acknowledged. I wanted adoration and gratitude and I was caught up in an idealistic romanticism, blinkering me to the cold, sterile reality of what this really was – a hook-up between friends.

Andre shuffled his feet awkwardly outside the hotel as he lit a cigarette and blew a column of smoke out into the frosty air. He looked different in the harsh, grey light of December. There was no soft lighting or filters outside.

At least he'd got some sleep. I'd lain awake all night contemplating the stark reality of newly single life, listening to a wannabe porn star snoring.

"I'm sorry, Emily, I can't get involved with you. It's not right. You are a married woman – you have children," Andre offered apologetically, before leaning down and kissing me gently on the forehead.

Strange, his moral compass hadn't stopped him from 'getting involved' the night before.

I'd heard his words clearly but my troll interpreted them for me: *"He doesn't want you. You're old. You're past your use-by date."*

Andre hugged me before turning away and heading home and he took the air from my lungs along with him. My stomach turned over, twisting in knots, a feeling I didn't understand yet it was familiar.

The bus ride home was lonely, my head pressed to the glass watching the grey pavements slide by. Tears fell silently, caught by my scarf. I felt ashamed, not empowered. I felt dirty.

Despite our disappointing first encounter, neither of us wanted to let go. We remained in contact and continued to pursue each other a few more times; illicit meetings often late at night when he had been out and called me up, a little drunk.

The sex wasn't any less clumsy or fulfilling but it wasn't really about the sex. I craved attention and I'd learnt that by offering him sex, I received attention in return. I felt *something*, albeit momentarily, and it was better than feeling rejection. But the attention only lasted about as long as his orgasm.

After each meeting, he reminded me how complicated our situation was: I was an older woman with two young children, not divorced and still entangled by marriage; he was a younger single man. It was never going to be anything, but for some reason it was hard to let him go.

ADAM

FEBRUARY 2012

A COUPLE OF MONTHS LATER, I WAS SITTING IN A LOCAL pub one Friday night with a new friend, Lucy. She was meeting some work colleagues and invited me along. She knew I was single and feeling lost at home on the nights my sons were with John. Lucy was beautiful, yet she had no idea of her effect on men, or women. She reminded me of Marilyn Monroe: blonde-bombshell curls and curves to match and they made men fall at her feet. But it was her energy that they also fell for; like a little lantern, she radiated optimism and warmth with an infectious giggle that drew you in and made you feel wanted. I felt safe around Lucy.

We'd enjoyed a few scandalous nights out, staying up all night and wandering home at daybreak. I had my first taste of alcohol with Lucy – mojitos and tequila shots. I didn't like the taste of alcohol at all, but I began to enjoy the way one or two drinks made me feel: relaxed, a bit more giggly and less inhibited. Lucy was a comfortable drinker though and effortlessly drank pints of beer whilst chain-smoking. Beer and fags went hand in hand. It seemed that smoking was a sociable event and we were never short of people to talk to in the pub smoking areas. Lucy's killer curves and blonde curls always drew attention. I enjoyed bathing in it and being by her side as it meant I was never alone. I wanted to be like her. She made socialising easy – it was to her; she wasn't even trying. I, on the other hand, felt like a fraud; an actress playing a role, badly.

Lucy's boyfriend Michael, worked with a young man called Adam, also newly single. Adam was suave and at just thirty-two, younger than me in both age and maturity. But it was his playful confidence that made him even more attractive to me. His strawberry-blond curls fell below his brow and when Adam laughed, which he often did, his eyes danced with a naughtiness that was captivating. A few drinks down amongst us all, I was pushed to sit on his lap, the two singles forced together.

"Has anyone ever told you how amazing your bum looks in jeans?" Adam whispered in my ear as his hand held onto my waist. I blushed at his crass compliment.

No. No one had ever told me I had a great bum in jeans. It was wide and flat, not luscious and curvy.

At the end of our evening, we swapped numbers and I waited for Adam to contact me, hoping he would but unsure if his interest in me was just drunken bravado. The cold light of a newly separated, older woman with children was a big turn off in my mind.

The next day, a text arrived: "*Hey, it was great to meet you. Would you like to go for a drink Tuesday night?*"

I texted back instantly: "*Hi Adam, that would be great. Shall we meet in the same pub again at 8pm?*"

Shit! That only gives me three days to lose some weight, I thought. *I will just eat soup this time and definitely no bread.*

I arrived twenty minutes early and sat in my car to watch Adam arrive. I left a comfortable ten minutes before heading in, mostly out of nerves, but there was also an unspoken dating etiquette that dictated you shouldn't appear too keen. I think I'd already blown that rule with my instantaneous text.

"Hiya, good to see you again." Adam stood up from his pint to greet me. "Do you want a drink? I got one in already," he offered.

I smiled. "Hi. Um, thanks. A lemonade please, I'm driving."

"Tell me a bit more about yourself. The other night is a bit of a blur." He laughed.

I told him about my life: moving countries, separation, divorce, two kids and my job as a waitress. Adam told me about the football he played, favourite bands I'd never heard of and a finance job I didn't understand. We had little in common but I was drawn to that difference.

After the pub came a club and by 2am I found myself lying on Adam's sofa half-clothed, being tenderly kissed. Adam slowly traced his fingers down from my breasts, over my newly pierced belly, seemingly not repulsed by it. Adam liked piercings. And my flat belly.

"Your belly is so sexy. How have you had two kids? It's so flat," he enthused as he traced circles around my belly button.

I left his place at 5am to get ready for work, leaving Adam wanting more. We didn't sleep together. Denying him sex felt powerful, but I didn't keep him waiting too long.

Standing in Adam's doorway, the nerves kick in. I ring the bell.

What the hell are you thinking?

Adam's taken the morning off work to see me. He lied and told his boss he has a dental appointment.

I'm wearing a long winter coat, buttoned up against the winter chill, and knee-high, black-leather boots with six-inch heels. Underneath the coat is black lace underwear and fine stockings held up by a basque, nothing else. Cliché I know, but I want this cliché for me, just this once.

Adam opens the door with the same cheeky grin.

I unbutton my coat and open it without saying a word.

"Oh fuck!" he exclaims.

Adam's expression makes standing here, freezing and half-naked in February, worthwhile.

It makes the soup-and-fruit diet worthwhile too!

Less than a minute later, it's over. I guess this underwear was too much.

"I'm so sorry, Emily. It's been a while," Adam confesses sheepishly. He's holding me in his arms. "My ex, Emma, had huge breasts, I mean, they were amazing," he says as he runs his fingers over mine, cupping my small left breast as if in comparison.

Some thoughts are best left unspoken by a lover – that was one of them. It should have been my cue to gift Adam a lesson on diplomacy, but instead I said nothing, unable to speak. Yes, my breasts were small and less than amazing. Adam was just confirming what I already felt.

That night I found Adam's ex-girlfriend on social media and scrolled through her pictures on her open profile. Emma did indeed have incredibly large, voluptuous, twenty-something breasts that sat comfortably in her glamorous dresses. She had no wrinkles. She probably had no stretch marks under those dresses, or self-doubts, either.

Despite the differences between us and our underwhelming first sexual encounter, I continued to see Adam over the next three months – secretly of course – once or twice a week. Our dates revolved around pubs, drinking, bars and sex. I feared being alone more than anything and I used Adam as a way to avoid that uncomfortable place. His company, and his body, became an addiction. I fell for him and foolishly believed it was love. And that he felt the same.

I didn't want to introduce my sons to this younger man, although on some unbalanced level I'd really hoped he was my next 'one', the one to replace John. But Adam had other ideas. He was offered a well-paid job in the corporate sector in London and was leaving the following month.

I was still so raw and vulnerable from John's departure, I became clingy with Adam. I asked him not to go, trying to convince him to stay for a life with me, but he didn't want that. The day he left, I cried on him, sobbed, and could see from the expression in his eyes, he was probably grateful to be moving 200 miles away from me.

Adam's departure felt like a death, the loss and rejection felt overwhelming at times. I couldn't bear to listen to music. It felt as if every lyric to every painful love song echoed my broken heart. Those songs had been written just for me, they were my story, and the words of lost love and heartbreak were unbearable.

DANIEL

APRIL 2012

"Johnson! What are you doing here alone?" Harry boomed loudly, a little worse for wear, this pub being his third one on a Saturday-night bar crawl.

"Harry!" I squealed with delight, happy to see a familiar face in the busy pub. It was another one of my 'nights out for one' evenings, sitting in a pub alone, sipping lemonade.

Harry was the biggest prankster – he was slightly older than me but had a humorous boyish charm. We had met through a mutual friend at her birthday party and shared a warm platonic camaraderie. He saw me as one of the boys and only ever addressed me by my surname. Everyone loved Harry.

Standing just behind Harry smiling at me, was his friend, Daniel.

"Daniel, this is Johnson. You two will get on, you're both into all that weird meditation stuff!" Harry laughed as he squeezed through the Saturday-night crowds towards the bar to get the next round in.

"Hi. Nice to meet you." Daniel smiled as he shook my hand.

I beamed. "Hi, I'm Emily. Nice to meet you too."

"How come you're here on your own then?" Daniel looked puzzled.

"I'm separated and my kids are with their dad tonight, so I thought I'd come out – you know, better than sitting at home alone." I smiled weakly. *I sound so boring.*

Daniel towered above me, strong, tall and mysteriously quiet. He seemed shy, not brash and appeared slightly embarrassed by Harry's crude introduction. "So, you like to meditate too?"

And that was the gateway to an interesting conversation, a real one for once, not empty chit-chat that alluded to a quick leg-over. Daniel wasn't drunk or pawing at me or expecting more from me. He seemed happy to chat and genuinely interested in what I had to say and that was very appealing.

We swapped numbers after an hour or so and when the boys moved onto the next bar, I headed home, my confidence tank refilled. That was a good night out alone.

I went to sleep hoping Daniel would text me and the next day he did. A week later, Daniel and I met for a drink and agreed to meet again the following week to see a band in a local pub.

Live music – a real gig. How had I reached thirty-nine years old and never been a part of this scene before? I loved music, always had, but had never been in a packed pub, surrounded by people jumping about in a makeshift mosh pit. Another first.

I still felt like I was acting the role of a sexy, confident woman. I didn't want to disappoint Daniel by letting the cat out of the bag and exposing myself as the lost and lonely woman I really was. I agreed to go back to his place after our date.

After it was over, we lay together.

"Mmm, I love this." Daniel caressed my stomach, circling his fingers around my belly button before placing his palm gently across my belly.

Just as well I didn't eat much today, I thought.

"Are you hungry?" Daniel climbed out of bed, pulling his dressing gown on, just about covering his muscular, tanned body.

"Yes, sure, I could eat something. What are you making?" I stretched my arms above my head. It was almost 1am and I was starving.

"Bacon sandwich?" he quizzed, smiling.

"Yes, that sounds good."

"Do you want me to help you?" I called out to the kitchen.

"No, stay there, I will bring it to you."

A little while later, I was lying in Daniel's bed, naked, eating a bacon sandwich. No man had ever cooked for me before.

Neither of us wanted our children to know, so it seemed best to keep the relationship quiet in the beginning. As with Adam, we met in secret, which made the meetings even more exciting. Daniel had a motorbike so I would jump on the back, gripping his waist as we sped off on adventures. He also had a van with a mattress in it and we would take off for weekends away and sleep in the back. Music festivals, pubs, clubs and alcohol – I felt alive!

One day, I was laying on the beach with Daniel, ignoring my dermatologist's advice from twenty years earlier, bathing in the warm summer sunshine in a bikini. A bikini – I'd not worn one since my early twenties nor bared my skin to the sun, but Daniel made me feel liberated and reckless. My forties were shaping up to be a decade of many firsts.

Daniel traced his fingers down between my breasts, over my belly button down to my pubic bone. "Your stomach is so flat. It's very sexy, just ... here," he whispered as he touched the line just above my bikini bottoms. It was slightly concave; an area that hinted of the secret bounty that lay beneath the material. What was it with these men and flat stomachs? Flat *was* sexy then. I was pleased that my regular diet of cereal and salad had finally paid off.

My sons were with their father every Tuesday evening and it was an unspoken rule that Daniel and I would spend those evenings together. But those evenings spent together were becoming more infrequent. A year into our secret relationship, things had begun to change.

"*Hiya, do you want to go out for dinner tonight? xx*" I texted around 12pm on my break.

I checked my phone at 2.15pm in the staff toilets. I could see from the app that he'd read the message at 12.16pm.

Silence.

"*Hi, did you get my message? I'm free from 5-ish. What time shall I come over? xx*" I knew he'd already got my text but I was playing dumb.

I checked my phone at 5.15pm after work. I could see he'd read the second message at 2.37pm.

Nothing.

"*Hi, everything ok? Shall we grab dinner?*"

Third-time lucky, I thought, *he must be really busy.*

Silence.

I called. Twice. It rang out both times.

"*Look, I'm childfree tonight. I'd like to go out and do something. Can you call me when you see this, please?*" I texted once again at 5.34pm.

This silence *was* his response.

"*Is everything ok??!!*" I was getting angry now.

The message was read at 6.14pm.

"*I'm busy tonight x*" he replied.

"Arrrghhhhh. You bastard. How dare you put a kiss on it!" I

screamed, launching my phone across the room and slumped into tears; angry at him, angrier at myself for waiting. Another wasted night in on my own.

If you have ever been ghosted by a lover, or indeed anyone you care about; you will understand how emotionally cruel the pain of silence can feel. Worse still, when you can see they have read your message and chosen not to respond; it's akin to voiceless gaslighting and it throws uncertainty on everything. It makes you believe you have done something wrong, something to deserve the silent treatment.

Too many occasions went by with unanswered texts, phone calls that rung out that never got returned and when Daniel did reply, sometimes I'd get the dreaded one-liner: *"I'm busy tonight."* The painful dagger would twist in my stomach every time. It never got any easier to be passed up for something else; something, or someone, better.

Daniel was never quite all-in. He'd kept a part of his heart back and it was hard to be around someone with an emotional fortress around them. Occasionally he would let me in behind those walls, especially in the beginning, and when he did, it was wonderful. However, we were still in a secret, on-off relationship eighteen months down the line and I was growing tired of being invisible. As soon as it was clear my feelings were developing, he backed away and fell silent.

We pushed and pulled against each other. I'd take a step back and tell him it was over and in return he would convince me to come back. I'd get closer and comfortable in his loving attention once again and he'd react by pulling away once more in panic. Daniel continued to drift in and out of my life but I waited around for him, grabbing the scraps of his time when he threw them at me.

I'm standing in a bar watching a live band, a vodka soda in my hand. Daniel is by my side. In walks Penny – I've seen her before, confident and bubbly, a girl about town. She's in a short, sleeveless dress and her tanned legs look incredible. She beams at Daniel, a familiar face in the crowded bar, and he reciprocates with a wave.

Penny heads straight for us and Daniel turns away to chat to her. I let them talk – I'm waiting to be introduced, but he doesn't. I'm invisible.

I bet he fancies her.

She's giggling with him. I know what she's doing, I've flirted before. I feel intimidated.

She's got a much better body than me.

I nudge in.

"Hi!" I smile, announcing my arrival.

They both look at me, surprised at the intrusion.

Who is she? Penny's expression asks without saying a word.

His face says everything. I've interrupted him: Mr Single.

"This is my friend, Emily."

Your friend? FRIEND?! Are you joking?!! What, a friend with benefits for sixteen months?

I'm not his friend, I'm his fucking girlfriend! I scream at her inside my head.

"Hi, nice to meet you, Penny. *Cheers.*" I smile, raising my vodka soda to this innocent blonde enemy.

During the following few months, I tried my best to win Daniel back over with constant text messages, begging, bribing, offering sex, weekends away. Nothing worked. An awareness of how many female friends he had threw me right back in the comparison game of my teens.

As a woman of forty-one years old, I was starting to show visible signs of ageing and became hypercritical of my own skin and in particular, my wrinkled face. Injectables such as Botox and fillers weren't widely available as they are today, and even if they had been, I would have been too scared to try them. Instead, I racked up an unaffordable debt on my credit card buying a facial treatment machine that stimulated my skin with tiny electrical impulses, plumping it and apparently reversing the appearance of fine lines. I doubled the number of recommended treatments each week, hell-bent on speeding up the process and looking more youthful. It was tiresome doing home-made facials three times a week, always underpinned with an edge of desperation rather than relaxation.

I spent hundreds of pounds on my credit card on a new wardrobe and shoes, money I could ill afford, and the pleasure of my purchases was short-lived. The novelty of a new pair of shoes meant nothing if I had no one to wear them for.

Daniel made another new female friend and as their friendship blossomed, our relationship slowly died. One final bitter conversation over the phone sealed its fate.

In an effort to move on, he blocked my every point of contact with him; I couldn't reach him by phone, text, email or social media. And I did try in those early weeks. I sent begging texts and emails, all of them remaining unanswered.

Daniel may have blocked me on social media, but his new friend hadn't, so I tortured myself daily, poring over her public posts of adoration for him and their new life together. I dissected every inch of her, scrutinising her features for flaws to tear her down, but she didn't have any. She was taller than me, slimmer, younger. Her breasts were bigger, her hair longer. She was a successful businesswoman. I was a waitress.

She had everything I didn't have. She had Daniel.

DEPRESSION
OCTOBER 2013

I SLIPPED INTO A DEEP DEPRESSION. I STOPPED WANTING TO live. I struggled to get out of my bed. I stopped eating. Sometimes I'd manage to force down a bowl of cereal before bed. It wasn't intentional dieting; I was in a deep state of grief. Thoughts of food found no room in my head, for it was far too filled with Daniel and this immense pain I felt. Having stayed at a constant weight for three years, I then began to lose it through pure self-neglect and the twisted voice in my head applauded the loss. It revelled in it. *Yes, Emily. Slimmer will make you happier. Slimmer will win him back!* it cried gleefully.

Daniel ripped away a piece of me when he walked away; at least it felt that way and I spent the next few months searching for the missing piece of me – not in pubs or clubs, but alone. But that solitude was unhealthy and quickly became a breeding ground for an already rampant troll. *It's your fault, you know. They all left you for a reason. You're so needy, Emily.*

I hated Daniel, Adam, Andre, John and my dad – I hated them all for not loving me, for not sticking around, yet I hated myself more. I was culpable for all their departures, or so my troll told me. Five men – one dad, one husband and three lovers had all left me. I was the common denominator in these equations. There had to be something wrong with me. All these men, except my dad, had told me at one stage or another during our time spent together that I was clingy and needy.

Months passed by, but Daniel was still a constant thought and his new girlfriend's social media was a constant reminder to me. I just couldn't leave it alone. Like a scab, I'd pick at my wounds, scrutinising their latest adventures together. I couldn't stop myself, despite how much it hurt.

My declining mental state was affecting my job in the restaurant and my boss had noticed. I was often crying and overly sensitive to criticism so when he pulled me into his office to mention my drop in performance and to offer support, I saw it as a reason to leave. I read it as I wasn't good enough at my job and leaving meant I could avoid his criticism for good.

Jobs were few and far between, but I wasn't in the right headspace mentally to commit to training in anything new. I was barely getting out of bed most days – my children were the only driving force to continue. Reaching the last eighteen pounds in my bank account with two sons to feed was enough of a reality slap around the face to do something, so I answered an ad in the paper for domestic cleaners and began cleaning houses. It suited me. I could work around the school run. I was good at my job – I'd been practicing the role since the age of seventeen.

My favourite client never looked down on me for being her cleaner. Others did, but not her. Olivia was a lovely young woman and she always welcomed me into the flat she shared with her boyfriend, Josh. We would often sit and chat before she left for work. Olivia had a set of weighing scales in her bathroom. It became my weekly treat – a sneaky weigh-in. I'd wait until I'd finished cleaning the bathroom, as the extra activity might mean I weighed less.

Sometimes I'd gained weight, so I'd try a little harder to eat less that week until the numbers got back down to where I felt they should be.

Olivia had a full-length mirror on a stand that sat by her bedroom window. The room caught the morning sunlight and would flood the room with a brilliant, white, no-filter light. I used to sit on the floor to clean the bottom half of the mirror. It was my only rest time during the three hours. Olivia must have sat there doing her hair and makeup – sometimes there were tell-tale remnants of foundation splatter. I would spray the mirror with cleaner and wipe it away to reveal my face and body. Sometimes I would look, sometimes I wouldn't. It depended on what the bathroom scales had revealed to me earlier.

When the boys went to John overnight, I would spend my evenings alone sitting in my bed, curtains drawn, a laptop balancing on my knee and a supply of chocolate around me. I would watch one romance movie after another, often crying and consoling myself with chocolate. The chocolate was somehow soothing and often the only thing I had eaten all day. I yearned for a man to hold me and kiss me, to love me the way the man held his leading lady in the movie. I was still aching for the fairytale.

I started seeking reassurance in my daily horoscope. I wanted to believe things would change and felt sure the answer lay in a generic horoscope on my social-media newsfeed. That became compulsive checking every day on four separate astrology sites and I would find myself waiting up until midnight each night just so I could see if the next day's horoscope offered me something more hopeful. The obsession soon bled into tarot-card readings. First online, then reading my own cards in my bedroom.

I would shuffle and spread the tarot cards over and over, sometimes for hours at a time, until I got the answers I wanted – Daniel was coming back to me and we would live happily ever after. I showed no respect to the craft of tarot and after multiple spreads, it was inevitable that at least one would hint at my perfect scenario. I was simply finding what I needed to find in the cards – there was nothing intuitive about it – but that alone didn't satisfy the deeply driven need to know my future fate.

"Hi come in, come in, sit down."

Sandra smiles as she leads me into her dining room. The windowsill is filled with crystals and an incense stick is smouldering on a sideboard. The fragrance feels rich and comforting. A salt lamp is casting a warm glow on this dull November afternoon.

"Have you had a reading before?" she asks as she shuffles a well-worn deck of cards over and over with experienced ease. I like her. She feels warm and motherly.

I smile back. "Yes, I have."

Actually, I've had five readings in the last eight weeks, but you don't need to know that.

Sandra explains how the reading will work and recites the 'only for entertainment' disclaimer, required under law, before fanning out a deck of tarot cards in an arch in front of me, face down.

"Pick seven cards for me and place them here. Whilst picking, I want you to think about something you want to ask me." She smiles.

Daniel, Daniel, Daniel, Daniel, Daniel, Daniel ... and ... umm ... Daniel.

He's the only reason I am here.

When the reading is complete, I part with forty pounds and leave, before bursting into tears.

She hasn't told me Daniel was coming back to me. They never do.

I replaced my food obsession with spiritualism and became addicted to psychic readings amongst other things, online and in person. It was an expensive addiction: at its worst, it was eight readings in eleven weeks. When what they told me didn't fit, I moved on to the next reader. I lied to each one, ashamed of my addiction, but it was as real as any other out there and one I kept to myself. It began with healing treatments and soon became an obsession with spiritual churches and psychic fayres, Reiki, crystal healing, angel healing, mediumship evenings, psychic drawings, aura readings, EFT, sound baths. Each offered me something, momentary peace, but it was always short-lived.

After my ninth psychic reading, one in which I'd spent most of the hour sobbing, I left feeling broken, knowing I couldn't go on that way. For one thing, I was hundreds of pounds down on a credit card I kept borrowing from.

I began to search for help online and stumbled across an Englishman based in America who was offering a foundation healing course. We agreed to have a chat on Skype and I cried for the entire hour. Unlike many of the other spiritual quests I had tried, this one was different. He didn't tell me Daniel was coming back either but he did tell me that after the course, his departure wouldn't hurt so much. It was a course that helped you address old emotional baggage and he could tell from our conversation I was holding onto years of grief. Daniel was just a trigger. It went way back, much further back than him.

A few weeks later, I completed the foundation course, emotionally lighter and much stronger than I had been in many years. It wasn't easy, there was so much suppressed grief over losing my dad and baby. I was scared to feel that grief again but I did, and it was necessary. That grief had made me cling onto Daniel, John, Andre and Adam – because I unconsciously feared losing them too. I saw that for myself, finally. I still loved Daniel, but it didn't hurt in quite the same way.

The addiction to spiritual courses and tarot readings, that desire to know my future fate, was fuelled by the need to control my environment as well as manage my grief. But after the course, the need to look at tarot cards, horoscopes or other props went. I could see life more objectively.

A few weeks later one Friday night, I bumped into one of Daniel's friends. She mentioned that Daniel had moved in with his new girlfriend. It still stung a little but it was pain I could handle – his departure no longer overwhelmed me.

The next night, a Saturday, I was in the house alone while the boys were both with John. I'd just finished the latest romance movie and with the credits still rolling, I opened a new tab on my laptop and dipped into the world of online dating – just a little window-shopping for single men, a little something to pass the time:

Paul _72

Divorced. Dad of two. Singer. Songwriter. Guitarist.

Interested in: Yoga. India. Music.

Seeking: A relationship.

Paul had dark, curly hair, a fit, athletic build and the kindest blue eyes I'd ever seen.

Should I message him? I wondered. *No*, I thought, slapping the laptop shut. *Fucking men. I've had enough of them!*

PAUL

2014

Three weeks later, I looked again. Paul was still there, single and available, so I plucked up the courage to message him. He replied later that night and soon we were messaging day and night.

6.05am: *Good morning, Emily. Hope you slept well and have a lovely day at work x*

12.07pm: *Afternoon, how's your day going? X*

11.03pm *Goodnight, Emily. Sleep well x*

And so many more in-between. We spoke about everything. Every subject.

Was this man for real? He was a responsive texter. He didn't play games or ghost me or make me feel second-rate. After another three weeks of text chat, we agreed to meet in a local pub.

"Hi Emily. It's so good to finally meet you."

Paul throws his arms around me and we hug comfortably,

like long lost friends. His skin is warm and soft, his arms feel safe around me, comforting and homely.

Paul beams. "I *knew* I recognised you from somewhere. I remember you. I remember that smile."

Our paths had crossed once, aged fourteen at an under-sixteens' disco but we never spoke. I didn't know he'd noticed me. Paul was one of the cool kids, a brilliant dancer. I was just Belly, the skinny girl with two left feet.

I wasn't looking for love, I was still nursing a fragile heart, but I believed the best distraction would be a little harmless conversation with a new man who seemed interested in my life. I didn't want anything serious, not a boyfriend or a husband, just a friend and someone to flirt a little with, no strings attached.

Paul was different to the other men I'd met. He was quiet, polite and an old-fashioned gentleman. Paul was also my own age, not a toy boy. His priority was not sleeping with me – it was the opposite and that made me feel safe. There were no lewd jokes or sexual innuendo. Paul wanted to get to know me, he listened to me and seemed to like me for the woman I was. For the first time I felt completely free to be me and not pretend or wear a fake persona to please him. Paul made me feel adored and secure in myself and not second rate to another woman in anyway. *Daniel who?*

I didn't want it to happen, I wasn't ready to fall in love, but I did. Paul took me out for dinner, we went to the cinema, for beach walks hand-in-hand. We spoke for hours. He brought me flowers every week. Paul dated me, he wooed me. He held my hand in public and he was proud of me. Paul introduced me to all his friends, his family. His sons.

Within three months of meeting, we had introduced our sons to one another and it felt right. My sons fell in love with

Paul's gentle nature as much as I had. And I fell in love with his sons. We became one big, blended family. That stability was something we all needed. We moved in together and though I vowed I'd never get married ever again; we got engaged the following year. Finally, someone *really* loved me.

A NEW BODY

2016

I WAS ON A CONSTANT DIET IN THE RUN UP TO OUR wedding in 2016. To be the perfect bride, I had to be thin, which I wasn't. I was curvy with big hips and breasts. The slim body I had when I met Paul had slowly become well-rounded.

I stopped eating anything from my 'naughty list' and weighed myself daily, scrutinising the natural fluctuations in my weight. At almost forty pounds lighter than I am now, I was considerably slimmer, yet I still wasn't happy with how I felt in my own skin.

Our wedding marked the end of that particular diet for me. Whilst other couples sipped the complimentary champagne with their delicate breakfasts, we didn't. Paul was an alcoholic in recovery and I could never drink in front of him, but there was nothing to stop either of us from hitting the all-inclusive buffet.

After a cooked breakfast, two rounds of toast and the obligatory but pointless visit to look at the fresh fruit display, I'd head to my favourite part of every morning – the pastries. It became a standing joke between us – mostly me mocking myself – how many mini pains-au-chocolat could I eat in one sitting. *Go on, Emily, get stuck in!*

One morning, I'd managed to eat eleven. I wrapped up several muffins and croissants in a napkin and slipped them in my bag to take back to the room with me, as if eleven pastries were not already enough. My mind told me to make the most of it whilst I could, for soon I'd be back on a post-honeymoon diet, so then pastries would be back on the banned list again. As was so often the case with me, if I deprived myself of certain foods, when whatever restrictive diet I'd been on had ended; those were the very foods I would eat to excess. I wished I could be that woman who eats a boiled egg and some melon at the hotel for breakfast, but I never have been her. It's always the beige spread for me: cakes, pastries and toast with lashings of butter and chocolate spread.

Within eighteen months of our wedding, I had gained another twenty-two pounds in weight and I found it extremely hard to accept my new, heavier shape. I was no longer the slim woman Paul married. Along with my weight gain, I'd become comfortable with Paul and through that comfort I'd become complacent with my style and self-care.

In the early days of our relationship, I made a concerted effort with my clothes and hair in order to look attractive; but when you fall in love, and you love someone deeply, the depth of love goes way beyond the superficial and I knew Paul loved every inch of me, with or without make-up or perfect hair. Somewhere through that progression in our relationship, my appearance became less about style and more about comfort.

Almost two decades had passed since my early twenties and yet I still wouldn't wear short-sleeved T-shirts or shorts and would camouflage my body with clothes even in summer for fear of showing my arms and legs. I couldn't even look at my own body, so there was no way I would reveal it to others, whether I knew them or not.

Paul's first wife was the opposite to me in every way. She was petite and athletic in build with toned, tanned arms and legs. Her blonde hair was always perfectly styled and her make-up equally so. I couldn't have been more different to her: curvier – much curvier –brunette and barely a scrap of makeup. And despite Paul's constant reassurances of his love for me, I still compared myself to his ex-wife. I'd dread bumping into her without warning, cringeing inside at my choice of casual clothes and lack of make-up if we met. I felt inferior; underdressed, under-presented and overweight.

I'd find myself seeking Paul's reassurance, disguised through feeble humour. "Well, you really got the opposite in wife number two, didn't you?" I'd joke, patting my fatter belly. But the fake smile hid much discomfort and shame. Maybe if I said it first I'd beat him to the insult and it would hurt less. But Paul never insulted me.

"Stop it, Emily, I love you, all of you. I love everything about you," Paul would reassure and that reassurance was comforting, if only momentarily.

As my weight crept up, I began to feel uncomfortable undressing in front of Paul and would get changed in the bathroom instead. I'd hurriedly jump into bed, only ever with low lighting on and I'd always sleep in pyjamas. I had regressed back to the days of covering myself up in bed with John. My 'single lady, sexy lingerie in bed' days were long gone.

My heavier weight was also a passion-killer. I could no longer let go and enjoy sharing intimacy with Paul. A part of me was more than a little absent; my mind constantly running an inner monologue of doubt:

Does my stomach feel fat underneath him?

Do my thighs feel fat to him?

Let's change position. Maybe I will feel less fat that way.

Why are my breasts so floppy? Can he see my stretchmarks?

Am I any good at this? Is he even enjoying it?

I wanted to enjoy sex and it felt *great* when I could shut the voice up, but the trouble was, the more weight I gained, the more vocal the troll became.

I didn't want to be thinking about how wobbly my tummy was or if my thighs felt fat to Paul in the throes of passion but it was *all* I could think of. That and how one breast was now migrating east and the other to the west, destination: armpits. What happened to my small, perky-breasted twenties?

Of course, Paul didn't care about my new, fuller figure, in fact he would always compliment me on it, but I simply couldn't accept what he was saying because I didn't *feel* that way.

WEIGHING SCALES

MARCH 2018

By my mid-forties, I had new husband, a new house, a new job, new stepsons – a completely different life – and for a while, things were going okay. Life was busy but peaceful.

By 2018, at the age of forty-six, I'd had enough of the extra weight I'd slowly gained and decided to join an online slimming group. I'd never tried organised diet clubs before, but other people I'd spoken to had found them supportive and their weight loss was visible. That was very appealing. But I wasn't confident enough to walk into a church hall and sit with a group of other dieters and there was *no way* I wanted to be publicly weighed! Just the thought of the humiliation made me shudder. An online version would be much more discreet. I downloaded an online slimming club app and skipped through the usual disclaimers without bothering to answer truthfully:

No, I don't have an eating disorder.

Nope, I've no history of eating disorders either.

Current Weight: I'll round my real weight down a bit. Less to lose that way!

It was difficult to begin with, swapping from oversized portions of pasta and bread to calorie-counting and weighing food. It was an eye-opener how much I was overeating according to the recommended amounts, especially the portion sizes of pasta, and it took some time for me to accept that I didn't need to eat quite so much. Certain foods were considered 'naughty' – crisps, chocolate, cake, doughnuts, sweets, amongst others – and best limited. I stuck religiously to the programme, recording everything I ate and drank for twelve weeks. It became an obsession.

The first thing I did every day from waking up was to plan out my allowable intake for the day, every mouthful meticulously monitored by me and fed into the app. I used every single calorie up. I filled up on salads, endless piles of watery salads, 40g of pasta a day and hardboiled pasty-grey egg yolks. Urgh.

Monday morning is my weigh-in day. My weekly treat.

Actually, I'm doing it daily, I just don't tell anyone.

I've been to the toilet. My pyjamas have been stripped off.

I'm gasping for a glass of water, but better not until I've weighed in.

I step on the scales, waiting anxiously for the double zeros to stop flashing.

Yes, I did it! I lost a pound since yesterday.

Actually, that's not that much. I don't understand, I've been so good.

Let me take my bra and pants off too. That will help.

I will just move the scales over here instead. That part of the floor is a bit lumpy.

I step on again. 00:00 is flashing. Hurry up and change!

Ah, there we are. I knew it. I've lost one pound, one ounce.

Every time I stepped on that weighing scale and my weight was a little lower, it felt so rewarding. I was back in control of something in my life when everything else around me was beginning to spiral beyond my reach.

I'd set my goal as 9st 13lbs: it had to be just under the magic 10st mark. This was a little over the weight I was when I met Paul: 9st 8lbs. It was the magic weight I hovered around when I weighed in each week on Olivia's scales. It was also the weight I was when I was with Daniel, Adam and Andre, one that made me feel better in my own skin. I needed to get back there.

I lost a substantial amount of weight during the three-month programme, hardly surprising given what I was eating, or not eating. During that time, I got just as much of a kick out of denying myself food as I had from eating it. The deprivation felt powerful, just as it had when I'd had anorexia decades earlier. It was as if reaching the magic number on the scale would bring me happiness. And it did, but only temporarily.

"You've lost so much weight!"

"You look so slim - you look amazing!"

Who wouldn't love a compliment, a verbal badge of honour for losing weight? We all do, right? But I clung onto these comments from well-meaning friends because they affirmed and reinforced my beliefs about being slim.

I took a picture of my feet on the weighing scales, proudly marking the momentous occasion. When the programme ended, I didn't renew it. Why did I need to? I had reached my goal weight and everything was grand. But of course, within a few months, life began to change.

BINGE

JANUARY 2022

YOU WEAK, USELESS BITCH – WHY CAN'T YOU JUST WALK away?

I'm standing on the high street opposite a supermarket. It's just me, my troll and I. We're just staring.

They sell my favourites here – cakes, doughnuts, biscuits, bread – my top-tier in binge foods. We are living separately now but Paul is sitting in the car waiting for me. He's brought me to a health-food shop to get a supplement. Someone suggested it might help me stop binge-eating.

The health-food shop says it's out of stock, they're ordering it in for me. It will be here tomorrow.

That's fine. I can start over then.

It's *not* going to beat me, not today. I can fight this urge.

I turn around and head back to the car but something stops me.

A familiar story starts inside my head: *I must* have another blowout. One final fling with food. Tomorrow is a new day, a new diet and I know things are going to be different this time, I *promise.*

A cake would be so good, I can almost taste it... So sweet, so sugary.

I can't wait to eat one. I need some, *right now*.

But wait ... I already hate this fat body I'm in. Look at me, I'm disgusting.

Emily, don't do this to yourself again.

Please, make it stop. Please just make this feeling go away.

I begin to cry.

I find myself inside, in the bakery aisle. A blueberry muffin to begin with, it's 420 calories. I know the calorific value of everything I eat, I count them every day, but honestly, who cares?

This is the last time. *I promise.*

Next, a coconut and raspberry loaf cake. It's my son Jack's favourite one. I will get this one for him, a fresh baguette for later too. I'll grab a lemon drizzle muffin – one will do – and a pack of four jam doughnuts too.

Okay, four cakes are enough for one visit. I haven't really got the funds. I'll take the shortest route to the till.

Please, no one stop and talk to me because I'm fighting back the tears.

One by one, I'm scanning my haul through the self-checkout.

I *can't wait* now. Almost there.

I'm outside the shop, the muffin box is already in the bin. I've torn the muffin top off, shoved it in my mouth and the blueberry goo is on my chin.

But honestly, who cares? This is the last time. *I promise.*

There it is, that feeling: sweet relief. That's the muffin done. The wrapper is in my pocket.

Quick, wipe my chin, the evidence must be hidden.

That relief is slipping away already; I need to chase it before it's completely gone.

I'm back in the car now, seatbelt on.

"I got some doughnuts; do you want one?" I offer.

"No thanks, you carry on," Paul declines.

Good, one more for me then.

One doughnut down and I'm licking the sugary aftermath from my lips. It's okay, this is the last time, I *promise.*

"Thanks for the lift, Paul," I call out, waving goodbye. I'm not lingering to chat today, I need another doughnut.

I'm just inside the door, eating number two, then three, before I stop to put my keys down. I pop my head around the lounge door. "I got your favourite cake today, Jack. Would you like some?"

Jack's eyes light up. "Yes please, Mum."

What I really want is to get stuck into this cake myself. Thanks for the permission, son. Coconut flakes and crumbs are falling everywhere as I shove it in. A third of the cake is already gone, I better give Jack some.

I throw the last doughnut in the bin. I don't feel so good now, I feel a bit sick.

Actually, I might as well finish that doughnut off first. It's the last time I'll ever eat one again, so I'd better get my fill.

I rummage in the bin. Found it! It looks ok, let me just brush the bits off. It's only scraps and wrappers, a bit of dog hair. There's no raw meat in there, so no harm done.

Number four is gone now. There, job done.

I fucking hate myself!

When I met Paul in 2014, I had no way of knowing I was Paul's new band-aid, something to cover his old wounds, someone to temporarily hold him together after his first wife ripped off a major one when they separated. He had lost both his parents in his late twenties and his two sons were the only thing holding him together when I met him; he gravitated towards my newfound balance and light. Underneath the papery exterior of a decent, loving man was deep trauma masquerading as a little harmless drinking and it was only a matter of time before it surfaced.

By the middle of 2018, serious mental illness had entered our home, devastating us all and it tore our blended family apart. Both of my teenage sons were struggling with anxiety and depression; the eldest gambling and the youngest developing severe obsessive-compulsive disorder. I was forced to give up my full-time job to care for my sons as they sat on endless children's mental-health waiting lists, deteriorating. Meanwhile, Paul secretly fell back into full-blown alcoholism. His sons stopped coming to stay and I was caught in the middle of it all, trying to shield each one from the other, and themselves. I told this story in my first book, *Pushing Through the Cracks*.

When Paul, Thomas and Jack started to deteriorate further, I slipped into the role of a full-time carer for three men with debilitating mental illness and that's when I found respite in food.

The bingeing began with me 'rewarding' myself late at night with a sweet treat, the occasional biscuit, or three, the odd chocolate bar or packet of crisps, until it slowly became all of those in one short sitting.

When I'd finally get everyone settled at night around 11pm, I felt I could finally breathe. I'd consider myself as entering 'my time', to really kick back and enjoy a well-deserved treat of some sort. I'd earned it, or so I told myself. Whilst many mums might pour themselves a large glass at night at 'wine o'clock' to help them unwind, I didn't. Instead, I'd head to the kitchen and prepare a sandwich, grab a packet of crisps and a chocolate bar too. I wasn't hungry, just tired and worn down. Food offered me a temporary pick-me-up.

I'd carry my little bounty of snacks back to bed, climb in, put the television on and finally relax. Paul would normally be asleep, so I moved with painstaking precision not to wake him. I didn't want to get caught eating all that food at night. Not that he would ever condemn or criticise me for it, but somehow him catching me would multiply the embarrassment of eating so late at night. Doing it on the sly also made it even more forbidden and rewarding.

I'd feel bubbles of excitement looking at my mini picnic set before me on the bed. I'd always start with the savoury items first, followed by the sweet. The moment I took the first bite or two, the excitement and reward dissipated and I'd eat the rest of the food unconsciously whilst distracted by the TV.

Food packaging became an unwelcome enemy when lying next to a sleeping Paul. Late at night, the sound of food wrappers seemed to amplify, a bit like someone rustling popcorn in a hushed cinema. As soon as I'd finished one item, I'd push the empty wrapper under the bed, out of sight. When Paul stirred, I'd freeze in my feeding tracks until I could sense he was settled once more, then carry on eating. Once complete, I'd feel a weird sense of satisfaction that I'd got away with it, mixed with guilt.

Slowly, the weight crept on from my night-time feasting. As things intensified at home and Paul, Thomas and Jack's mental health continued to decline, I slowly found myself using food more often to escape my emotions. It was as if food gave me a release from my feelings. When I was angry, I'd head straight to the kitchen and rather than vent or release my anger as I'd been shown all those years before on the healing course, I'd bite through it, literally. I'd pick crunchy foods – biscuits usually, despite the fridge full of carrots – and angrily chew on them whilst having imaginary rants in my own mind. Crunchy foods satisfied something in me and temporarily hushed the anger within me. Of course, the food didn't alleviate the emotions at all – the quick fix was an illusion and instead, it made things far worse.

Around the same time, during the summer of 2019, Paul moved out of the family home, finding himself in crisis and struggling with alcoholism. I encouraged him to go, convincing him it would be better for him, but in reality, it would be better for me. I wasn't coping with life at all and I knew that once he was gone, I would have no one around to see my night-time feasts and no one to hide my behaviours from, which would make them that much easier to execute.

What began as an occasional binge response progressively developed into a default habit as a reaction to stress. Soon I was eating large amounts of food several nights a week. I began to plan the binges, feeling excitement at the thought of eating. It was as if I was preparing for a forbidden event and in the early days, I felt a heady anticipation of eating all the foods I'd denied myself for so long. Just the smell of the food caused excitement; as I ripped open a pack and the aroma hit my nose, butterflies danced in my stomach and the eating would begin, soon becoming frenzied. The foods I chose to binge on were those I'd spent a lifetime putting in the naughty corner of food, the food sin bin: chocolate, cake, pastry, ice-cream, biscuits, white bread, sweets, popcorn, crisps, doughnuts, cereal and toast with chocolate spread. Those were my go-to foods every single time, each one processed and high in either sugar or fat, or both.

The volume of food I began to consume was alarming. I'd often restrict food during the day and eat barely anything until dinnertime. I'd congratulate myself for getting through a whole day with eating very little, for resisting the cravings, but this food restriction was often a guaranteed prelude to a binge. Once night-time arrived, I couldn't stop the overwhelming noise in my head that encouraged me to binge. I'd get so angry at myself for ruining another day of restriction that could have resulted in weight loss if only I'd just been stronger, if I'd just stopped myself. Other times, I'd have a healthy breakfast, lunch and whatever dinner I was making for the boys. But afterwards, despite being satisfied and comfortably full from dinner, I'd still binge.

It would begin with the craving for something sweet so I'd eat a chocolate bar from a multipack. But one no longer satisfied me and I'd pick out another one, convincing myself it was ok, because they were slightly smaller in a multipack. But as soon as I started the second bar, the voice would begin: *You've ruined your day of healthy eating, so if you're going to do it, go out with a bang, Emily!*

And with that mindset, I granted myself permission to let loose and gorge myself on all the forbidden treats, because behind the consent to binge was a resolution that the next day would be different. I promised myself I'd never do it again and would return to sensible eating once again.

I rip the outer wrapper from the multipack of chocolate bars.

They're only treat size so it doesn't really matter. Two of these are just like one normal bar, right?

I tear at the wrapper of bar number one with my teeth. It's quicker. The familiar smell of chocolate barely has a chance to hit my nose before it's pushed in my mouth.

Melting fat and sugar coats my tongue.

I *love* this taste. Ah and here it is, sweet relief.

But it's not enough. Number two is gone, then, three, four and more, until all six are gone. In less than three minutes.

Shit. What have I done? No turning back now.

Quick, drink some water as my teeth and tongue are coated in chocolate, sticking together.

What next?

Wait. Stop... Is that Thomas? Shit, don't let him see all this.

I freeze.

No, it's okay, it's just the dog.

I make two cheese sandwiches, with lashing of real butter. I need to be able to taste it.

You've really done it now, so spread it on extra-thick, Emily. Can you see your teeth marks in it?

Two packets of cheese-and-onion crisps pushed in between the four slices of bread. The thick butter holds every crumb in place. I pour myself a large glass of orange juice, swigging some to help push the sharp crisps and stodgy white bread down.

Now what?

I open my bag of binge goodies and poke around. A family pack of cheesy snacks now. I can't eat these slowly. The snacks don't go in one by one – it will take too long.

I use my hands like a scoop and shovel a load in my mouth. Almost full, my cheeks are bursting ... another swig of fruit juice. There, that softened the snacks. I swallow hard. Cheese and orange juice mixed together. Urgh, I can taste the heavy oil. I knew I shouldn't have bought these cheap ones.

I glance at my phone. 10.57pm. Plenty of time.

Heartburn... It's a bit early for this. Let me grab some antacid.

I swig on the thick chalky liquid and it helps. It's pushed that burning heat down, for now.

Now what?

Sweet popcorn, a 500g bag. The kernels are sticking in my teeth. I tip the bag into my mouth to get every last one, even the unpopped hard ones. I'll spit them in the sink.

Yes! I've been waiting for these.

I tear open the box. It's been just enough time to melt the ice-cream a little. I like it melted., it's easier to eat. Three chocolate caramel ice-creams, one by one.

This is making my teeth ache.

Swirling around in my stomach is a milky popcorn, cheesy snack, orange-juice concoction. I rub my belly. It hurts. I feel sick. I start to cry, but I am not done. I can't stop this.

Now what?

Four bowls of cereal. I love the feeling, the sound of the crunch.

I hate my life; I hate who I have become. I don't want to be here anymore. They're better off without me.

Family cheesecake next. I take a dessert spoon out of the kitchen drawer. I can fit more on it. I use it to push past the smooth sickly strawberry cream and scoop out the hard biscuit base. It's my favourite. Well, one of them.

I rub my belly. It hurts. I feel sick. I think I'm nearly done.

What shall I finish with?

Two bits of toast. The butter swims on the bread. Now for the chocolate spread, yellow and brown swirling, glistening.

Two don't touch the sides.

Just two more. Okay, maybe four.

Now, I'm done.

Fat, useless bitch. Look at you! Look at what you've done.

I'd eat it all within an hour or two. It hurt my body. My stomach would swell uncomfortably from the volume of food I was eating. My teeth would sometimes ache from the sugar. The toast always heralded the end – quite often, it was the final food.

All the food had to be consumed by a deadline before midnight. Midnight was my food curfew, the magic sweet spot that brought a new day and the promise of a new beginning without bingeing. The binge-free days became few and far between and the feelings of self-loathing, of disgust and feeling weak became as much a part of the bingeing as the food. The frequency of bingeing increased until it was happening several nights a week and alongside was an increasing sense of loss of control. I felt powerless to stop it.

I remember going into my local supermarket. I'd go in there most days and knew most of the staff – hardly surprising given my frequent visits during the height of my binge phases. Of course, no one knew. No one questioned someone buying food in a food shop. If I'd been buying two carrier bags of wine or beer several times a week, they may wonder what I was up to, but I was no different to any other shopper. It was, after all, a grocery shop. The difference between food and any other addiction is you can't avoid it like you can alcohol and drugs. You can't simply abstain from food for life.

I'd often go in the early evening when the reduced items were laid out. I knew the best days to go, the quietest, and would walk there in storms or on rainy wintry nights when not another soul would venture out, just because those nights would guarantee me more choice. I was almost certain to find a dessert, a trifle or cream cakes reduced amongst the sandwiches and wilted vegetables that looked long past their best. There was always a trolley with reduced bread and pastries, so I would load my basket up with doughnuts, packaged cakes and biscuits – whatever was discounted and sugary. Somehow the cheap price heightened the pleasure of the binge and lessened the guilt of the money I was wasting. The bargain price also encouraged me to buy far more than was necessary. Neither of my sons wanted piles of cakes and biscuits going out of date but I would trick myself into believing that I was also buying it for them. The discount sticker confirmed it for me.

Sometimes I'd try to divert attention from my basket at the checkout, convinced that the checkout operator was scrutinising my food choices whilst scanning them. "It's not all for me you know. Teenage boys – you can't fill them." I'd roll my eyes in mock irritation of my two sons and their supposedly hollow legs.

But the reality was neither Thomas nor Jack would get a look in on what was bought. I always kept the bags hidden, sometimes in obscure places including the downstairs toilet and under the kitchen sink where they wouldn't venture.

There was always a sense of excitement for me at the till, because paying for the food signalled the feeding was getting close and the anticipation was momentarily thrilling. I would feel nervous and fidgety knowing it was going to start and hoped the queue wouldn't be too long.

Once I left the shop, I'd allow about ten metres before diving into the bag and beginning. It was all strategically planned, out of eyeshot. If it was a box of six cakes, I would open it in the carrier bag so no one could see and could have eaten three by the time it took me to get home – a five-minute walk away at most.

It was almost a feeding frenzy. The sugary deliciousness started a reaction. One was never enough and it felt as though something was inside my brain, taking over. It wasn't unusual for me to eat a bag of four doughnuts one after the other, sitting on the wall or walking home. I didn't want my sons to see them and selfishly, didn't want to share them either.

I'd usually split the binge food purchases between three local shops. I knew which favourites of mine each shop sold and buying a few items in each shop felt less conspicuous. Living opposite one shop and ten metres from another, one of which opened until 3am, was both a convenience and a nightmare. It allowed me to keep topping up with more food. The thing with my bingeing was sometimes, I just wasn't done. I simply couldn't satiate the craving enough, despite my body's discomfort. So, I'd head to alternate shops and pick up an extra bag of sweets or chocolate or crisps. Sometimes it would be three trips and by the third I'd have to make up an excuse and would often buy a household item or benign packet of dried herbs chosen at random just to detract attention from my next snack. Would the shop assistant even question my actions? Probably not, though I guarantee if I'd gone in three times during one hour for cans of beer they may have.

THE EATING DISORDER CLINIC

2019

By now the bingeing episodes were frequent – several times a week – and by that stage, I felt a complete loss of control over my behaviour. Not only that, but my physical health was declining. I felt nauseous and lethargic. It was not surprising given what I was eating.

I was filled with good intentions of stopping and would sometimes throw food in the bin just to stop myself from overeating, but it wasn't long until I began taking food back out of the bin and that behaviour reinforced my self-disgust. What kind of person eats food out of the bin?

Me. I'd become that person.

During a binge, the fourth consecutive one that week, I searched '*bingeing lots of food*' online and came across an eating disorder on a health website. It was called binge-eating disorder (BED).

I was pushing down the last two pieces of toast with chocolate spread as I read through the list of possible behaviours associated with BED. I opened my mouth but nothing came out. It was a silent cry of pain. I slid down the kitchen cupboards, still holding my half-eaten piece of toast. The chewed chocolatey goo fell out of my mouth onto my arm as I curled on the kitchen floor, sobbing.

I was familiar with all the behaviours on the list: I ate when not hungry; I ate quickly and huge volumes of food; I ate in secret; I felt so much shame and self-disgust; I felt out of control.

"Emily Johnson?"

I look up from my phone.

"Hi, come in, come in. I have a student doctor with me today who will be sitting in on our consultation. Are you happy for her to remain? "

"Yes, that's fine. I don't mind." She looks just a little older than Thomas.

The doctor is leaning up against the examination couch, arms folded. The student doctor is sitting down with a clipboard.

My doctor knows Paul. He was the one who helped him when he began drinking. My doctor knows Thomas ... and Jack. He knows all the family history. He knows I've been spinning plates. Does he know they're crashing down around me and I feel so alone?

"Now, how can we help you today?"

Don't cry. Don't cry. Don't cry.

"Um. I think... I think I have a problem with food," I whisper.

I've never said those words out loud before, to anyone. I feel like a child; a useless one for wasting the doctor's time over something so trivial.

"I see. Can you tell me a little more? In what way do you feel you have a problem with food?"

"I can't stop eating at night."

I feel so ashamed.

Big fat tears appear and I can't stop them. I wipe them away with my cuff of my coat without even attempting to hide them.

"I see. How long this has been going on? Can you tell me what you eat at night?"

I list off the previous night's binge, like some shameful shopping list of forbidden foods.

Ground, please open up and swallow me. This is so embarrassing.

He doesn't flinch, nor scold me, nor call me fat and useless. Instead, he smiles with his eyes, warmly.

"Well, I think what we have here, Emily, is just a faulty part of your brain. You see, you've been under an enormous amount of strain, haven't you? Given your history with anorexia, I'm going to refer you to an eating-disorder clinic for some support. They will assess you and take it from there. Now, I need to get your weight for the referral. If you can pop your shoes off..."

"I know how much I weigh," I interrupt.

You're not weighing me fully dressed. That would be a lie.

"I thought you might," he confirms.

My doctor referred me to an eating-disorder (ED) clinic at the local mental-health unit. I left his office in floods of tears; not because this man was the first person I'd confessed every sordid food detail to, but because through the referral, I recognised I was struggling. And now the one person who was propping up three other family members with serious mental-health issues, had succumbed to her own mental-health disorder. I thought she was stronger than that. I thought she *should* have been stronger.

The referral was pre-Covid so the wait was mercilessly

short at just three months. I sat in the clinic's waiting room with other men and women, some my age, some much younger, filling out a questionnaire about my eating habits. We were all different shapes and sizes, but we all shared a similar facial expression – lost.

My treating doctor was lovely and I spent the hour with her recounting my lifetime obsession with my weight, diets and food and the beginning of it all, which appeared rooted in the anorexia of my teens. I was diagnosed with binge-eating disorder and given a self-led recovery programme. I had to work through a book.

Whilst there was relief in having a diagnosis and treatment plan, I was very scared too. Part of the programme was to work towards only weighing myself weekly, instead of daily. That alone felt overwhelming, but it also encouraged me not to restrict food groups or diet. It was at odds with ingrained patterns I had been adhering too for most of my adult life and I was terrified of relinquishing the control I thought I had. I was also gently warned I may gain weight to begin with, apparently not uncommon when you stop restricting food and lessen the binges, returning to more normalised eating.

I didn't want to hear that. I wanted to hear I would lose weight. I thought this was all about my weight, but of course, it really wasn't.

We had fortnightly phone calls to check on my progress with the recovery programme which felt reassuring, but I still didn't really understand *why* I was bingeing nor how I could have gone from one eating disorder as a teen to another that was the extreme opposite.

The programme did help, when I stuck to it, but it required commitment, daily monitoring, planning and record-keeping of everything I was eating, drinking and thinking about food. These were all things I had done before, but this was different:

it was balanced, non-obsessive recording of the details and without the guilt.

But my family life was in chaos and I couldn't prioritise my own health enough to stick to it. Then Covid-19 arrived and everything ground to halt, my doctor was off sick and I saw the pandemic as the perfect excuse to bail on my treatment because my family were in crisis.

They needed me more. My own recovery could wait. It wasn't long before the bingeing returned.

DEPRIVATION & CONTROL, AGAIN

JULY 2020

As the months slipped by, I was in a living mental-illness hell. All four members of our family were struggling. Paul and I were separated; he was in the grips of alcoholism and depression; Thomas was addicted to online gambling and anxious; Jack, whilst waiting for treatment, was spending hours a day repeating OCD rituals. I was in survival mode. I wasn't really sleeping, I was existing. Everything in my world was dangerously out of control so I returned to long periods of diet and deprivation in an attempt to control the only thing I could: food.

In-between periods of bingeing were days, occasionally weeks, of restriction and this was one of the fundamental causes that underpinned my bingeing. The old 'good' and bad' food labels were still there from my teenage years. 'Bad' foods were the root of all evil in my head. They led me to the point of no return many times and it was often after periods of sustained bingeing. I'd feel so ill, I'd vow to never do it again and avoid carbs and sugar completely. The decision to diet then gave me an enormous sense of control over something.

I'd pretty much been on one diet or another since I was thirteen years old but when I reached my forties and BED had begun, they became more frequent. Once I withdrew from treatment at the ED clinic and the bingeing episodes returned, the diets in between became more extreme. I'd go on drastic detox diets which in themselves were unhealthy and very unbalanced. They always recommend that you seek medical advice before going on crash diets but of course I never did. If I'd done so, I would have been advised against it, especially with an active eating disorder.

These detox diets were often fad diets too; highly restrictive with very few calories and eliminating entire food groups. They made me feel very weak and the headaches I'd suffer from cutting sugar overnight would leave me feeling wretched. The only thing that encouraged me to sustain such strict diets was my obsession with how much weight I could lose in a day. And when I say obsession, I truly became fanatical and began weighing myself sometimes as many as fifteen times a day. My behaviour around the weigh-in ritual escalated. I would hop on the scale once, note the reading, then go to the toilet and come back and try again because, as ludicrous as it sounds, I believed I'd weigh less after passing urine. Better still, a bowel movement.

I'd repeat the weigh in several times until it gave me confirmation of a lower weight. If the scales faltered and gave a different reading, a fraction heavier, I'd keep on weighing myself, moving the location around the floor praying the numbers would reflect what I hoped they would.

If they didn't, I would feel utterly deflated and resent the fact I didn't accept the lowest reading when I had the chance. It was ounce fluctuations, quite possibly caused by low batteries and old scales, but to me, they were critical. I had to remove the batteries every day from the scales in order to prevent me continuing to weigh myself throughout the day. It was remarkable how those digital numbers on a lump of plastic sat on my kitchen floor could rule my life, but they did. Those numbers wielded such power over me – they could either make or break me every single day. They had for years.

My most substantial weight loss was nine pounds in a week on a detox diet. Of course, very little of this was actual fat. I had starved myself and ate little more than salad and fruit after days of sustained bingeing so in effect, what I lost was mostly water. As soon as I returned to a healthier eating pattern, a few of those pounds returned. Extreme diets were an exhausting loop to be caught in and kept fuelling the cycle of deprivation and bingeing.

"One, two, three, four .... five."

Ok, go on then, you can have ten today.

"Six ... seven, eight, nine, ten." I slide the salted pistachios into a pile and wrap them up, ready to savour later.

"Hang on, I should weigh them to double-check." I unwrap them and pop them on the kitchen scales: 12g.

"No wait, I better take the shells off first, otherwise the weight will be wrong."

I remove the pistachio shells and pop the nuts on the scale: 7g.

"That's better. Right, let me double-check the app, make sure they are the same."

"Okay good... So that's ten nuts: 34.42 calories. Not too bad."

I applaud myself for being sensible with this high-fat, 'bad' snack. This is my treat for the day. I log the ten pistachios on my calorie-counter app.

"Okay, that leaves me 1465.58 calories today."

Time to plan the rest of the day.

1500 is my magic number. Not one single extra calorie is allowed.

After one drastic detox diet, I purchased a calorie-counter app for my phone and that became the next unhealthy infatuation – counting calories and weighing everything I ate again, as well as myself. For a while it distracted me, but it soon became my new obsession.

I would sit in the app forums, poring over the posts written by other dieters every day, trying to glean from them all their tricks for successfully losing weight. I wanted weight loss results and fast! I had about three stone to lose to reach my 'goal weight'. I lost half a stone and got a reward badge, then some months later, the reward badge for losing a stone. But the satisfaction was short-lived, because the next two stone awards were still sat there on the app taunting me, a daily reminder of how overweight I still was. I began restricting my food intake before weigh-in day just to hit the weekly targets I'd set for myself. If I didn't hit my target loss; I'd give it another day or so of eating virtually nothing and try again.

Along with the calorie-counter app, my step-counter became its best friend. If I didn't reach the recommended 10,000 steps a day, I'd feel like I had failed my self-imposed goals. Reaching that magic number felt imperative to maintaining my weight loss, rather than something to improve my health and fitness. It made me feel successful and verified my self-discipline. If I couldn't fit the steps in throughout the day with actual walking, I found tangible ways to hack the step count.

Hanging onto the kitchen bench with both hands for support late at night was my easiest and most frequent. I'd step from side to side, one foot to the other until it hit the mark, always before midnight. Only then, once completed, could I go to sleep.

CHEW AND SPIT

AUGUST 2021

"Emily, would you like to go out for dinner next week? My treat!" Paul enthused.

"No, not yet, but by January next year, I should be at my goal weight. Then I won't have to worry about diets ever again!" I laughed, but this was no laughing matter. I was deadly serious, sadly.

During this calorie-counting phase, Paul, from whom I was still separated, asked me if I'd like to go out for dinner for the 'Eat Out to Help Out' programme. In August 2021, the British government had subsidised businesses to offer half-price meals on certain days, to encourage people to come back out and jumpstart many failing restaurants. We were trying to repair a broken marriage amid our family's chronic mental-health problems. A simple meal out was a grasp at some normality.

Paul was taken back by my response. To him, it was extreme, but to me, it was normal. He was used to me recording calories. Even if we sat having a coffee, I'd log the calories and sugar sachets and note the dent the coffee had made in my permissible intake for the day. I'd have to adjust the rest of the day, so I didn't go over my limit. But recording calories was one thing; putting off going out for a meal for five months because of numbers on a scale was another. To Paul and to most balanced, rational people it was inconceivable, but this was my reality. I genuinely believed that the magic 'goal weight' would bring my own personal body nirvana and freedom from a lifetime of diet stress. Being slimmer would make me happier.

After ruining yet another diet with a forbidden croissant, I made a silent vow: *By my fiftieth birthday next year, I WILL be my goal weight again.*

In the height of this calorie-counting phase, if I bought my sons a pack of blueberry muffins, I'd set myself one aside and begin to eat it, in secret. Only this time, I would chew the cake, allowing it to melt in my mouth, long enough to taste the sugary butteryness and blueberries, before heading to the bin and spitting it out. *That's one way to have your cake and eat it, Emily!*

It wasn't the first time I had chewed and spat food out. Whilst growing up in London, I was forced to eat school dinners at long trestle tables every lunchtime. Leathery, bitter-tasting pigs' liver with shredded cabbage and watery gravy made me wretch, but the teachers forced us to eat it, pacing behind us with rulers ready to slap the table, ensuring we ate our sloppy feed. I quickly learnt to put small bites of whatever foul-tasting food was on the menu that day in my mouth to satisfy the teachers, then spit it discreetly in my hand, before flinging it under the table, as far away as possible from me.

I couldn't swallow the blueberry muffin, for that would mean going over my allowed daily calorie intake, something deemed unacceptable to me. By spitting it out, I could enjoy the pleasurable taste and sensation momentarily, without the fear of gaining weight from it. I would repeat the chewing and spitting routine until the muffin was gone. This behaviour was only reserved for cake, doughnuts, biscuits and bread. Not surprisingly, these were the foods I would deny myself during those days.

Nevertheless, I was in a better place in my life. Things were starting to improve at home. Both my sons were emerging from their mental illness and Paul was sober. And I was in control of my food intake once again. More importantly to me, I had lost weight and people had noticed.

One afternoon, I popped into my local supermarket. Whilst browsing for fruit – a welcome change from my carb fests – Steve, one of the staff who was around my age, stopped me to remark on my new slimmer body.

"You're looking so well!" he exclaimed. "You've lost so much weight! Well done! Good for you, love!"

"Thanks!" I beamed back, patting my belly, clearly delighted that all my hard work and deprivation was paying off. I *had* lost weight and others could see it.

I walked off with a spring in my step and my basket full of healthy goodness, smug in the knowledge I was on the right track *finally*.

Within three months I had lapsed and returned to sustained bingeing, regaining all the weight and another stone in addition. It would make me squirm inside every time I saw Steve, convinced he'd noticed my weight gain and was disappointed in me and my larger shape. If I saw him stacking shelves, I'd divert to another aisle, certain he was checking out my basket's binge contents and thinking to himself, *Uh huh, she's back at it again then!* with a disapproving tut under his breath. Of course, Steve wasn't doing anything of the sort, but my troll convinced me he was.

I re-referred myself to the eating-disorder clinic – it was clear I needed to get some help again. I was warned it may be a very long wait.

TOP HEAVY

OCTOBER 2021

Sitting on the floor in the loft, I'm surrounded by clothes that no longer fit me. It's depressing. I used to have a body that fit into these. I used to be thirty, too. Will I ever fit back into these size eights? Maybe ... just maybe, I will fit back into them one day. I can't bear to part with them though. They remind me of happier times. Slimmer times. I stuff them back in the bin bag, angrily and toss it down the hatch to the landing below.

Dream on, Emily. You're a size sixteen and even those are tight now.

I come downstairs. It's daily weigh-in time. I step onto the scales. I know it's going to be bad. I've been bingeing almost daily for weeks. I can't fit into any of my clothes.

Hurry up and get this over with.

My heart sinks: 13st, 8lbs. A personal best.

Gold medal for your highest weight ever. Fucking hell, Emily!

I go back upstairs to get dressed. I catch sight of myself in the landing mirror.

I can't bear to look. I can see the outline in my peripheral vision. That's enough.

I move the heavy wooden unit across the mirror. The black bin bag with clothes of my former body can go on top. No need to look at *this* fat, useless body anymore. I'm too disgusted.

"Thank you for letting me join the group. I've been bingeing for almost five years. When I was a teenager, I had anorexia. Now I have BED. I was diagnosed in 2019. I've tried everything: diets, Keto, slimming groups, calorie-counting, weighing my food, macro-counting, juicing – even throwing food out and nothing is helping. Night time is my worst time. I try to be good every day but I can't stop the overwhelming feeling to binge and I hate myself for it. I'm the heaviest I've ever been and it's making me so miserable. Has anyone overcome this and do you have any tips? Thanks."

During a prolonged bingeing phase, I joined some BED support groups online, anonymously. It's a lonely disorder and one that carries so much personal shame, so seeing other people experiencing the same awful thoughts about themselves as I was day after day, was comforting in some strange way. It was also incredibly sad because I knew their pain.

Sometimes I would read posts of hope – people who'd found a way out of their hell and I'd feel happy for them and hopeful for my own recovery, but often I'd feel jealous too. I wanted their escape from the chaos; I wanted it to stop, but honestly, most of all, I wanted their weight loss. That was the solution to all my problems and when I reached my magic goal weight, none of this would matter anymore, right? Wrong.

Binge-eating disorder can't be seen. It doesn't come in one body size, neither does it discriminate against gender, age, ethnicity nor financial status. The people in the support groups were from all walks of life yet all the stories were the same. We all shared the same cry: *I hate my body. I hate myself. I feel out of control. Someone help me – I just want to make this stop.*

In October 2021, I caught a virus. It knocked me off my feet for two weeks. What started off as a flu-type virus morphed into a gastric bug in the second week and I was very unwell for about seven days. Unable to stomach any food at all, my weight dropped substantially. Despite feeling utterly wretched and crawling from the toilet to the landing to sleep – heading up the loft steps to my bed felt overwhelming – that troll was quietly clapping its hands in glee. *Yes, you may feel like death, Emily, but you're losing weight!*

Who on earth can find celebration in redecorating the toilet bowl with yellow acid filled diarrhoea hour after hour, for days on end? Me.

I had scheduled an appointment with a respected homeopathic practitioner some weeks before and the appointment happened to coincide with my recovery from the virus. I wanted to see if he could give me any advice on the binge-eating. During my visit, I was connected to a SCIO bio-feedback device by five straps. The machine measured electrical impulses sent back by my body connected to a wire on my wrist. One of the results indicated that I was a poor methylator.

Simply put, methylation is a biochemical process that the body goes through which enables the reproductive, neurological, cardiovascular and detoxification systems to perform their necessary functions. Two functions stood out to him in my test results: the regulation of hormones, in particular oestrogen and the production of dopamine. Could it be possible I was seeking a dopamine high, that pleasurable reward from the sugary foods I was consuming? In addition, my oestrogen levels were showing as particularly low. My periods had been absent since my late thirties – something I'd neither investigated nor worried about given my gynaecological history. It was easier for me to mentally attribute the weight gain to my age and hormones, rather than acknowledge it was also down to overeating and lack of exercise.

The two foods that my body showed an intolerance to were grains and refined sugar. Hardly surprising really – I'd been abusing my body with both for four years. The practitioner suggested I try some simple changes in my diet, taking a range of vitamins and a supplement called inositol – a type of sugar – which would help my body regulate the methylation process, in turn helping to balance my hormones and dopamine, amongst other functions. The supplement was added to my list of things to sort one day. That could wait for another time.

Later that month, I self-published my first book, *Pushing through the Cracks* – a memoir chronicling four long and difficult years living with my family's mental illness and addictions (and my own, despite my denial). My challenging life as a mother and carer was temporarily lit up with trickling sales and each encouraging new review. As I buried myself in learning fresh marketing skills and threw myself back into the world of social media, my mind was distracted and once it published, I rode on the crest of a dopamine wave for several weeks. I was getting my feel-good fix from social media.

I didn't even think about food and I wasn't conscious of its absence, which is quite remarkable given my usual obsession with it. I just ate when I remembered or when real hunger growled in my belly – a feeling I hadn't known for a long time. Bingeing excessive amounts of food with relative consistency for four years had altered my conscious perception of when I was either hungry or full. Fullness had never been a factor in preventing a binge. I binged regularly past the point of full, into discomfort and pain.

As the initial hype surrounding the new publication started

to settle, I slowly slipped downwards again and relapsed spectacularly in the run up to what for me, is *not* the most wonderful time of the year – Christmas. The bingeing was back. Just because I had published a book didn't mean that my life was all smooth sailing. The same issues existed. My family were still struggling with their mental health. And so was I.

BURNOUT

JANUARY 2022

In the new year, I felt I had no choice but to increase my work hours. Life was becoming increasingly expensive in the UK; fuel and food prices were rising and without a doubt, worrying about money was affecting my mental health. I had never been unable to pay my rent or council tax before but I found myself in the uncomfortable position of not being able to afford either and making phone calls asking for a stay of execution from further action. Thankfully, both organisations were very understanding but it was clear I would need to increase my hours to make ends meet going forward. Working full-time and caring for my son meant my working week was seven days long and back to eighteen hours a day between my roles.

As if from nowhere, I started to feel unwell; not sick with a cold or flu or bingeing hangovers – this time it was exhaustion, pure fatigue. I would go to bed, sleep eight hours and still struggle to wake up the next day – and when I did, felt just as tired. No amount of sleep was helping. I was dragging myself from my bed to begin my day, my body feeling heavy and achy, and the exhaustion made me weepy.

The strange thing was that Jack was improving very slowly,

Thomas was getting on his feet and I'd finally accepted I couldn't fix Paul or my sons. The truly horrific days had passed, I was sleeping normally again and could finally see light on the horizon once more. So why did I feel exhausted now?

I stopped showering or washing my hair – neither seemed a valuable use of the little energy I had. The weepy feeling intensified and the slightest comment, pleasant or otherwise, triggered emotional meltdowns of epic proportions. It felt as if every nerve in my body was fried. The increase in working hours and fear around money was unsettling me and the bingeing began intensifying.

Sitting in the kitchen crying, I called into work sick, barely able to string my sentences together. My employer provides access to a counselling service – they'd been incredibly helpful in the past so I called them. I lasted a minute or so into the conversation before breaking down.

Grabbing my coat and phone, I headed outside onto the street. I needed space to let the emotion out and somehow strangers on the street hearing my distress was easier than my sons or neighbours doing so.

Sitting on the side of a busy junction, I sobbed to a stranger at the end of the phone for forty minutes. It was hard to breathe. The counsellor agreed to refer me for face-to-face counselling, something I had never had before.

The idea of counselling felt hopeful. I had always kept a little bit of the story back from everyone, not fully revealing what was really going on in my world out of shame. It had been a relief to be transparent about everything with an anonymous voice at the end of the phone. The counselling was scheduled to start a week later.

My counsellor, Catherine, was a warm, welcoming lady in her sixties who instantly put me at ease. She had a lifetime of counselling experience under her belt, along with a lot of lived experience. No matter what I confided in her, she listened without prejudice. Catherine soothed me with her compassion and empathy and sometimes we strayed from my feelings to our shared life experiences. There was comfort in that too.

During my first session, Catherine asked me for a timeline of my life. Often our life issues are rooted in our childhood experiences, so it was important to go back to the beginning. I reeled mine off with ease – it had only been four months since I had published my memoir, so my experiences were easy to recall. Catherine confirmed what I had experienced was a lifetime of small trauma. It was difficult for me to accept. I had always defined trauma as experience of huge, horrendous events such as war, death of a child or perhaps a murder. I had not experienced these things. I just saw my life as a series of experiences that had toughened me up, part of life that had to be endured but Catherine disagreed. She said my life had been a series of many small traumas that over a long period of time had become overwhelming and had been affecting many aspects of my life.

I described my physical symptoms of exhaustion, the constant tearfulness and feeling like my nerves were fried. She suggested it was 'burnout' and recommended I see my doctor. I thought burnout was a phrase you use when you felt tired, not a medical condition. How could I be suffering burnout now when I was sleeping again? Why not a year earlier when I was barely functioning on just two or three hours sleep a night?

Catherine explained that my body had probably been running on adrenaline and coping with sleep deprivation during the most difficult years, but when life normalised a little for a me, perhaps my body was letting go and catching up with much-needed rest.

I looked forward to my weekly appointments with her. It reminded me a little of the confession box at church, but without the punitive prayers for my sinful thoughts. I felt I could safely say anything to Catherine, and I did, even the darkest thoughts I had kept to myself all those years. She just listened. I didn't have to filter my feelings and I liked that. It was like having a motherly figure to talk to, but one with emotional detachment and someone who didn't overlay her comments with judgements or opinions.

"I don't understand why I couldn't call him Dad. It's like I couldn't say the word. It was stuck in my throat and I just couldn't say it," I told Catherine. This had sat with me for years.

"Well due to his absence both physically and emotionally, you didn't identify him as your dad. That's possibly why you felt that inability to address him as your dad."

It was so simple really but knowing why didn't take away the guilt.

With Catherine's help, I started to unpick some of the little traumas so I could understand the impact they'd all had on me. I wanted to know *why* I developed anorexia and why I had been so fixated on my body shape and diets. But most of all I wanted to know how I ended up with another eating disorder, one that this time made me overeat.

I booked in to see my doctor and barely made it through the door before bursting into tears. He knew of Jack's history and of Paul's issues too and it was clear from my floods of tears I was way beyond coping. The doctor signed me off work for a month and recommended full rest. Easier said than done – I was still a full-time carer and living daily with serious family mental illness behind the scenes.

Over the next couple of months, food kept me company once again. Lack of money became a new and unwelcome trigger. It was Easter weekend and I could hear people outside laughing and enjoying their day whilst I worked my shift. The kitchen window was open and the faint smell of barbecues wafted in.

I'd been able to ignore two text warnings of going into an unapproved overdraft all week, down to my last couple of pounds in my purse and ten days to go until payday again. I was living in a state of fear, borrowing from relatives whilst trying to play catch up for old debts that kept returning to haunt me month after month. I'd delayed the rent and council tax payments but the lack of money triggered regret for all the money I had wasted on binges. That made me want to binge even more.

After my shift ended, I headed to the local supermarket and searched the discounted food until found some reduced doughnuts and chocolate-mousse trifle desserts, a steal at just ninety-one pence for them all. That was the last of the money in my purse almost gone. Never mind, I could always borrow some more from someone.

Instead of heading home, I sat on the wall by the bus stop and began to cry; sad, lonely tears dripping down. There was no sound, just tears, and I couldn't stop them. I didn't know what I felt; overwhelmed by life again I suppose and alone. Food was my best friend.

I began eating the doughnuts, one by one until all four were gone, all in under two minutes. The soft sugary sweetness comforted me despite the tears. This money should have gone in the electric metre, not in me. None of that mattered in those moments though.

Once home, I ate two of the desserts back-to-back and burst into tears once more. Why did I do this to myself? Why couldn't I just stop this behaviour? Then I ate three chocolate bars I'd hidden from my sons and two packets of crisps. I felt full, bloated and my stomach ached uncomfortably.

I'd kid myself that if I didn't have those trigger foods in the flat I'd be okay, but that was a lie. It was a lie because I'd gone out of my way to buy them once again and they hadn't made me feel any better. They didn't resolve my feelings of sadness or my money worries.

The next day was no different. The urge to binge all day was so strong, I borrowed ten pounds that night from Thomas, with the sole intention of bingeing. I lied and said it was for the electricity metre.

Worthless human, my troll said.

I'd taken my son's money just to scratch a food itch that wouldn't go. I had food in the house and could have cooked something, yet it was processed carbs I needed. Sugar and carbs were the only thing I craved. It's hard to describe the intensity of the craving, though from what I'm told, it's like any other addiction. You think that food will ease or fix something inside you that hurts, though you don't recognise it as emotional pain at the time. It feels like you'd cut your right arm off just to satiate the overwhelming need.

"I fucking hate you!" I was shouting at both myself and the food I was about binge on.

I burst into tears, pushing the first blueberry muffin in my mouth in between sobs. It didn't even taste that good. That's the irony: none of it tasted that good. It wasn't about taste; it took away my pain, temporarily, but just as fast as I shovelled the food in, the feelings of self-hatred rushed in and filled my mind.

One chocolate Easter egg, four doughnuts and three blueberry muffins, two bags of crisps and three pieces of toast dripping in butter and chocolate spread later, it was nearly over. But not quite.

Just before 11pm I got dressed again and headed to the local shop. I knew when they all closed. I knew exactly where I could go to get my next fix.

I bought a family bag of crisps from the shop opposite – they were my favourite, crunchy and loaded with the salt and fake cheese flavourings that made them moreish and easy to devour in one go. I also bought a bag of cheap popcorn, a bar of chocolate and a carton of fruit juice with the change from Thomas' money, along with a packet of toilet rolls to cover my tracks and legitimise my late-night purchase.

I skipped the five or so metres back to my flat and kicked my shoes off, throwing the toilet rolls into the hallway. I didn't make time to put them away, instead heading as fast as I could to my space in the loft, hiding the shopping bag behind me in case Thomas appeared. I never wanted my sons to witness this gluttony.

I jumped into bed and laid out the food next to me, put a movie on my phone and began: the crisps first, followed by popcorn and the chocolate. The drink helped to push the crisps down. It's not easy to eat dry food lying down.

The familiar heartburn began halfway through the popcorn, most likely from my position in bed, not the food – that would come later. It was usually the day after that the indigestion and diarrhoea would start.

Once all the food was gone, I threw the wrappers on the floor and rolled over to sleep at 11.58pm. Right on cue. I'd made it just in time for my eating curfew.

The binge was over. I was no happier, no less broke – poorer in fact, because now I owed my son money too.

The next morning, I rolled over in bed and something dug into my side: a lump of stale popcorn. I'd missed that one. A reminder of what I had done the day before returned, along with the familiar poisoned feeling. A dry mouth, dehydrated from the salty overload and heartburn and a bitter taste coating my tongue.

I lay there crying gently. No sounds or sobs, just tears silently falling at my own poor choices and inability to stop them the night before. The powerlessness I felt to stop was one of the hardest parts to cope with.

Pulling myself up, I tied the empty wrappers into the shopping bag, feeling the need to hide the evidence from myself, if no one else.

"Well, you did it again, Emily, didn't you? It's a new day, start again..." I sighed loudly as I scolded myself and got dressed.

Whilst the dog ate his breakfast, I stood and stared at the pots of vitamins on the kitchen shelf. The lids were covered in a blanket of dust gathered from the months they had sat there, untouched. It was my 'Shelf of Good Intention', one that housed the vitamins I never took, along with chia seeds, hemp seeds, protein powder, dried seaweed and every other nut, seed and supplement I bought with every diet I could never stick to. They were all purchased with the best of intention for a new healthy way of eating that was always completely ruined by caving in and eating a slice of cake, or three.

But this is it! This time will be different, I have to start looking after myself.

Resolution number 134,769.

"*Buongiorno, Signora...*"

Carlos beamed as he tipped his cap with old-fashioned chivalry. His charisma and handsome appearance defied his sixty years of age. Carlos was half-Somalian, half-Italian and had a command of several languages, often greeting me in Italian when we met in the street.

I smiled back, slightly awkwardly. "*Buongiorno*, Carlos." Language wasn't my strong point, but I'd remembered some basic phrases from my summer spent in Italy.

Tony, the owner of my local shop, was busy telling Carlos

how his family were all sick with a cold. Carlos suggested he try his grandmother's cure: hot water, lemon, ginger and a clove. I pulled a face at the thought of drinking stewed cloves, but it reminded me of the advice I had been given by a doctor many years before.

A decade earlier I had travelled to India and decided to see an elderly ayurvedic doctor. After a slightly unusual examination of my tongue, skin and pulse, he informed me that my digestive system – my 'pipes', as he called them – were clogged through my Western diet of refined white flour. He suggested I drink warm water every morning with fresh ginger and lemon, to cleanse my digestive tract. He also recommended a course of several enemas at the clinic. I declined the latter, but his advice of drinking the bittersweet elixir remained with me. I had stuck to it for two years upon my return. If he thought my pipes were clogged back then, what would he say now after four years of bingeing?

It seemed no coincidence I should bump into Carlos standing chatting to Tony about the merits of ginger and lemon tea in the morning. Maybe the universe was sending me a sign to clean my pipes once again.

"*Ciao*..." I smiled at them both, faking enthusiasm I didn't feel and left the shop with a lemon and some ginger. My system felt poisoned and even the thought of my regular morning coffee turned my stomach.

Throughout the day, as I sipped my lemon-ginger concoction, I kept weeping. This latest lapse had really knocked me off my feet.

Later that day, I went to see Catherine. I had one session left with her and it was perfect timing. I wanted to gain a better understanding as to why I kept lapsing and why it felt beyond my control. Aside from the physical-health impact and financial cost of bingeing, I found the loss of control over my actions very disturbing.

Catherine and I spoke a little about my childhood and the feelings I had attached to food; those memories of my mum bringing me two slices of toast in bed with lots of golden melted butter and chocolate spread. I still, forty something years later, remember feeling her love through that warm toast. She would sit on the side of my bed smiling at me, stroking my hair away from my eyes as I ate the toast. It still gives me a sense of warm contentment when I eat it.

During my bingeing phase, I could never stop at one or two slices; I'd always feel sad as I took the final bite and I didn't want to reach the end of the experience. It had always been a minimum of four slices, sometimes six, and when the third or fourth slice was gone, regret replaced the contentment.

Catherine confirmed that I had formed patterns of using food to comfort myself in times of severe stress. She reminded me that this was just a lapse, not the end of my world. It was just a blip and it was okay to see it that way and move on. Catherine told me to be kinder to myself. For me, that was a work-in-progress.

My sessions had come to an end with Catherine but I could have carried on. We seemed to have only just scratched the surface of my disordered eating; there was always something else that surfaced or a current challenge in my life that that swallowed up our time. I missed those chats with Catherine.

THE BIG ONE

APRIL 2022

In 2021, I'd set an intention: to be my ideal weight for my fiftieth birthday. But that elusive goal was some three and half stones away and no matter what drastic diet I planned on going on, even I knew that goal was now unreachable in under three months.

Turning fifty was something I'd been dreading. It was a milestone, a big one. I was half that age in my head and I wanted to be half that age in reality ... and half the weight. It felt like my whole life hinged on this number. There was something terrifying about turning fifty – a harsh reality slap across the face that I was almost certainly over halfway through my life; that it was probably all going swiftly downhill thereafter.

In April 2022, I received an email advising my first book had been shortlisted in an award for independent authors and it would mean travelling to London for a ceremony at the London Book Fair. I burst into tears with excitement and a sense of relief. I had always wanted my family's story to count for something, for there to be a purpose to the difficult years. Maybe this was it; maybe being shortlisted validated it somehow, validated me. I'd taken the self-publishing route and it was a hard slog. I didn't have a publisher backing me or marketing and social-media skills.

After the initial buzz of excitement from reading the nomination email, old familiar thoughts flooded in. And soon those thoughts were on my lips and out of my mouth as I spoke to my dog, Billy.

"Oh Billy, I'm actually going to have to meet people. I'd better lose some weight!"

I ran to the downstairs bathroom, flicked on the light and leaned into the mirror, inspecting my grey hairs and my skin. I bit my teeth together and pulled a wide grin, assessing the stained shade. Everything about me looked old, tired and faded. Everything looked grey, wrinkled and yellowed.

You look old. You are old, I said to myself. *You are overweight. Your arms are fat. Your stomach is fat. You are fat. You are not good enough as you are. They will judge you on your appearance.*

"Well Billy, I'm going to need to dye these greys. I can't go like this!"

I had two weeks to lose almost four stones, sort my greys, iron the wrinkles and whiten my teeth. Oh and find something to wear that actually fitted.

And so began a drastic diet: grapefruit, eggs and salad. Zero carbs, not much of anything.

I held off going clothes shopping. That task could wait until I'd lost some of this weight.

I FORGIVE YOU

APRIL 2022

I WAS CONFIDING IN MY FRIEND, STACEY, HOW I WAS ON A crash diet for the award ceremony. She offered me a Rapid Transformational Therapy session, something that had been recommended at the start of the year by the counselling service, to help me address the lack of self-love I showed towards myself. Stacey knew of my family's mental illness and knew how much I beat myself up over the binge-eating. She had offered to help me before in 2020, but at that time I couldn't even carve out the time needed to help myself.

During a conversation, I told her how I could feel a physical twist in my stomach whenever I felt rejected by someone, anyone, it didn't matter who. I was so easily wounded by people's comments and took everything so personally.

Once again, she offered me the therapy and I declined. But this time she framed it differently and offered it as a gift for my upcoming fiftieth birthday, reminding me that if I kept refusing gifts from the universe, they may stop appearing!

I agreed and prepared for an early morning session as Stacey lived in Australia. I needed to ensure I had peace and quiet and would be uninterrupted by the dog or my sons, so we agreed on 6.30am.

A week later the session began and I was still a bit sleepy, so it was easy to let go – surrendering to hypnosis is key for this therapy to work. Stacey took me through a series of steps into a state whereby I would access my subconscious. I was awake with a level of awareness but undisturbed by sounds too – I heard the bin lorry driving past but it didn't bother me. The sound felt like it floated past my head.

Stacey guided me to find a place where I felt abandoned and rejected. It wasn't easy to begin with, it took a little time, but I found myself standing in my bedroom in my childhood home in London. It was strangely familiar – the yellow walls and my bed in the corner with pastel, candy-striped, flannelette sheets. It was hazy, as if I was looking at an out-of-focus photograph. It was dull in my room despite the yellow paint; it felt heavy and the window was closed. I couldn't see out of it.

Behind my bedroom door stood my dad – he was hiding from me. I felt his awkwardness. This wasn't a game of hide-and-seek – Dad was hiding because he didn't know how to be with me. That's one of my few memories of my dad – him hovering behind doors, as if he wanted to come in and be part of our family life but didn't know how to.

Stacey told me to bring him out from behind the door, so I saw myself stretching my hand out to him – it was me, but I knew it was me as a little girl.

I wrapped my arms around his waist as he towered above me and then as I did so, I started to cry, but the tears didn't wake me from this state nor memory.

With Stacey's guidance I spoke to my dad: "I understand, you know. I love you... I have always loved you... You are my dad; you have always been my dad... I forgive you."

In between each sentence were sobs – real tangible

emotional pain and my stomach started convulsing with waves. I could feel that familiar twist I'd feel at the sign of perceived rejection and it radiated up with the sobs until my body settled and I sighed deeply.

I sat my dad down in front of me and held his hands. I brushed his curls from his eyes and felt an overwhelming sense of love and forgiveness for him. Of course, I wasn't speaking to my dad in the here and now, he'd been dead twenty years, but I was pulling that memory out and reframing it, healing it in my subconscious mind.

Stacey guided me further back. This time I was about five years old, sitting in the same bedroom drawing stick figures of my family. My dad was a stick figure to the far right of the picture.

Stacey gently asked me what was happening, how my brother and mum felt about my dad. I could feel my mum's emotional labour – I could feel her pretending to be a happy family when my dad returned. I could feel Ryan playing alone in his room feeling sad that he didn't have his dad around.

Stacey asked me to bring my family together in my room for a big hug, I pulled us all in a circle and we huddled together, then I saw myself in front of my desk drawing a new picture – this time my dad was in it.

I turned around and the window was now open and the net curtains in my room were blowing in with the breeze – the sunshine was flooding my room. I had reframed the memory.

From nowhere, a thought appeared just after and I kept it to myself: *You don't need to binge, Emily; you were just trying to fill this hole.* We hadn't even addressed my bingeing or body image during that session.

Next, Stacey steered me to a more recent memory of rejection. I found myself standing in front of Daniel. Now I had his captive attention.

"You hurt me," I cried, my face twisting with pain. "You made me feel worthless and I am so angry at you for that." I felt the anger and I spat the words out. "You made me feel like I wasn't good enough. You really hurt me."

I sobbed and once again I felt the spasms in the depths of my stomach, only this time much milder. And then something odd happened – I found myself almost smiling at the realisation. "Wait ... this was never about me not being good enough for you. You were in pain too, weren't you? Now I understand. Daniel, I forgive you."

I came round from the experience, shocked that over two and half hours had passed. I felt tired and nauseous but I knew that something profound had happened and the nausea was the shifting of something deeply buried within me.

My loft space had no window or natural light, so I usually used my phone light to get dressed. That morning I stopped in front of the small mirror, looking at myself in the harsh white phone light and smiled. I didn't look down and pat my belly with my inner critic or recoil at my shape as usual. *This feels different!* I thought.

I headed down the ladder and went to the bathroom, pulling my long hair into a messy pile on top of my head. Peering in the bathroom mirror, I leaned in closely and examined the grey hairs framing my temple – it had been several months since I had been to the hairdressers. I looked at the fine lines, the wrinkles that line my forehead, a new horizon for every decade lived. I smoothed my fingers down my temple, caressing over the grey hairs and down across my cheek.

And then something quite unexpected happened. Out of nowhere I blurted out loud, "You are enough!" Not as a weak affirmation hoping to trick myself into believing it – I *felt* it. It was a declaration. A statement to myself.

That day felt different, lighter, as if I had unpacked a

heavy load I'd been carrying. It was subtle – I couldn't put my finger on what felt different, but *something* did. When I walked Billy, I wasn't shrinking down on myself as usual, hiding away and hoping no one would see me as I walked; instead I held my head up. I got through the entire day without realising that I had not thought about food. I didn't feel the urge to binge quite so much – I just felt peaceful inside. The days continued that way and the subtle feeling of peace remained.

A week or so later, I decided it was time to find a dress to wear to the awards afternoon. It had been five years since I had treated myself to any clothes other than the necessary cheap knickers and leggings from a fast-fashion store. I lived in black clothes for most of those five years, mostly out of convenience and comfort, but also because black echoed my life and mood at the time.

I went into the loft and uncovered another black bin bag of my favourite colourful clothes from a decade before. They were of another time, a period of freedom post-divorce and fun encounters with men. They were from a time of three stones lighter too.

Nevertheless, some of the dresses were made of forgiving stretchy material and I convinced myself they were worth a try. I stripped down to my mismatching undies and pulled attempt number one over my head. It became wedged on my shoulders, but with some wriggling I got the summer dress as far as my breasts. And that's as far as it got.

I pulled it off, laughing to myself as I peered into the label. "Size eight. Ah Emily, are you kidding?!" It went on the 'I will fit into these again one day, in my dreams' pile.

The next one was a comfortably large maxi dress, its heavily floral pattern perfect for covering up all my wobbly bits. I'd never worn it – it was one of those impulse buys in a sale. It was designed for a much taller woman and was at least two inches too long for me.

I turned to the side and looked at my profile. This dress covered the bumps and rolls of flesh and would be passable with a denim jacket covering my arms.

"That's a 'maybe'," I confirmed out loud to myself.

I sat on the floor going through the clothes in the bag, one at a time, each outfit evoking a memory of a different time and a memory of a body I no longer had. Yet rather than berate myself for my extra weight (the usual narrative) I felt acceptance. I was no longer a size eight, ten or even twelve. I was comfortably a fourteen to sixteen and that was the way things were. I had an eating disorder, one that had made me gain weight this time.

The following week, I ventured to a nearby shopping centre and made a beeline for the discount-label store. I found a loose-fitting long dress with long sleeves – my favourite kind – and headed to the changing rooms.

I undressed in front of the full-length mirror without looking, conscious my reflection was there, but it had been a long time since I had looked at myself in all my glory with fluorescent lighting. Let's face it – fluoro lighting isn't the kindest choice for cloakroom cubicles. That stark cold light is best reserved for the doctor's office and a cervical smear.

I pulled the dress on over my head and it barely made it past my breasts before I felt suffocated as it flattened them uncomfortably to my chest. It was a pointless to try to wriggle it down any further, so I grappled it off once again. I chuckled to myself: *In another lifetime, Emily.*

I headed to a nearby department store and straight to the sale rack. Hidden amongst the lines of winter frocks were two that caught my eye, both full-length with long sleeves, tighter at the bust flowing out at the waist to accommodate my hips.

These were right up my street. This was the style of old Emily, pre the 'black rag era' of the last few years.

I strode to the changing rooms, confident at least one would fit. The lighting was more forgiving in the changing room: a warm, soft white, not operating-theatre bright.

As I stripped off to my underwear, I paused and this time I looked. In the absence of a well-lit room or uncovered full-length mirror at home, this was something I had avoided for a very long time, way before the bingeing started. I cast my eyes over my arms and legs, arms whose appearance I'd hated since I was a teenager and legs that were dimpled, untoned and iridescent white from not seeing the sun in years. These limbs served me every single day, yet I constantly criticised them despite their hard work for me. My body was a different shape, my stomach no longer flat, with more than one roll of extra unwelcome flesh.

I spun around to look at my bottom and turned back. I finally saw me. I didn't hate it. I didn't spit bile at the reflection. Granted, I didn't like my shape, I still wished it was slimmer, but mostly I just felt sad that I had spent so long, years in fact, being so unkind to myself.

This is who I am. Right now, I said to myself.

I put the first dress over my head and pulled it down. It held my breasts gently and lay over my curves. It pulled in at the waist, the one I still had, and rolled out over my hips and down to my ankles. It didn't drown me in fabric nor strangle me in restraint. I looked up and saw me, Emily, and a beautiful dress. I bought the dress and the other one too. Both flattering my newfound curvier shape.

Cinderella shall go to the ball. Well, the London Book Fair at least.

By the time I left the shop, it was early evening and my stomach was growling with hunger. It wasn't a feeling I'd experienced for a long time. I'd learnt to eat regularly, for if I didn't, I'd usually grab bread for an instant filler and I'd never stop at one slice.

I'd gone most of the day without eating and that was a mistake because my hunger sent me into a large supermarket and straight to the cake counter. There were so many healthy choices I could have made – a sandwich or readymade salad – but the need for instant sweet carb gratification won. That and if I'm honest, a part of me was in mourning for a shape that had been replaced by a much fuller one in the mirror.

I bought two cakes and headed for the bus stop and as I sat waiting for the bus, I ate one after the other; a lemon-filled muffin first, followed by a sickly chocolate tart. Neither tasted that nice. It was often the case. The thought of the food was often more appealing than the actual experience.

I hopped on the bus and lost myself in my phone to pass the journey, along with everyone else. I sat scrolling on social media, my newsfeed filled with diets, anti-ageing miracle serums, Botox and lip-filler clinics, breast-enhancement surgeries and fancy-clothed perfectly made-up women or young, slim models in bikinis. Between the reels were adverts for underwear that contoured curvy women into a shape that society considered more acceptable. *Maybe I should get some...*

A sinking feeling came over me. I was about to turn fifty. I had just bought two dresses four sizes bigger than I used to be because I couldn't fit into my perfectly beautiful clothes anymore. A familiar feeling crept in and I turned my phone off, glancing out the bus window at the grey pavements sliding by in the dusk light. The tears fell, silently.

I got off the bus and headed to the mini supermarket near home. I knew it was coming but I resigned myself to it. I was tired, hungry and unsettled. The cakes had started something and it wasn't done. And so, I stocked up on the old favourites. No one batted an eyelid. Why would they? There is nothing unusual about a woman buying a bag of groceries. Only this bag was solely for her, for one sitting.

Sometime later, a bowl of pasta, a whole baguette of garlic bread, two bags of chocolate and a cinnamon cake down, I was done. My stomach was uncomfortably full and painful. It had been some time since I had eaten that way. This wasn't a huge binge and unlike every single other one before it, I accepted it had happened. I did not pull myself apart or torture myself. There was no negative self-talk. The aftermath was very different this time.

That night, I went to bed with a half-eaten bag of chocolate buttons beside me. I'd had enough after two other bags before that one and had resealed it. That was unlike me. My usual mentality was finish it all, clear all temptation out of sight because the next day would be different.

As I rolled over to one side and welcomed my old friend, stomach ache, I knew things could be different and I resolved to make the changes I needed to make; not for the numbers on the scale, not this time, but because I was fast approaching fifty years old.

This was the decade my dad had died from cancer and his dad before him, both far too young. Longevity didn't run in that side of my family. I was no spring chicken and carrying round extra visceral fat around my organs with a history of family heart disease and cancer was pushing my luck.

The next day I contacted Stacey and told her of my binge, slightly disappointed that it had happened after my realisation under hypnosis.

She reminded me that we hadn't worked on the eating disorder – just the feelings of abandonment and rejection which fed into the lack of self-worth. The bingeing behaviour was something entirely different. That was for another session.

Stacey asked me to explore how the binge had felt, what my thoughts were afterwards and how I felt now that it was over. Other than the physical effects of the regular food hangover, I realised I *did* feel different this time. I felt a sense of acceptance that it had happened and a resolve to be more conscious of ensuring I ate regularly and well. I wanted to be kind to myself which was a new and unfamiliar feeling.

A couple of weeks later I was on my way to London. I missed the bus and there were no taxis available for twenty minutes. I scrambled a neighbour to drive me to the coach station and made it with just moments to spare. Within minutes of getting on the coach, I had eaten all my lunch I'd packed. It was only 9.03am.

I got lost in London but after two tubes – one in the wrong direction – one train and a bus ride, I eventually found my way to the London Book Fair. I was late and I'd missed the talks I'd planned to attend.

Arriving, I felt like a fish out of water. Surrounded by large stands and hustle and bustle, it was the first busy environment I'd been to since the Covid-19 pandemic. The place was heaving with authors and publishers from the international book world. I was just a mum who'd written a book that was shortlisted for an award. Big events were not a part of my usual world and these were not my usual people. I felt like an imposter.

I bought the most expensive slice of stale cake I've ever eaten and headed to the wall at the side of the hall where the awards were taking place. I slumped down on the carpet. My feet hurt. It was the first-time I'd squeezed into my knee-high heeled boots in four years and I was really regretting my footwear choice. My calves had doubled in size since I'd last worn them and they pinched just zipping them up.

"Now moving on to our final category: memoir and autobiography. Congratulations to all of our finalists for these four outstanding entrants. The judges have thoroughly enjoyed reading them. And the winner of The Selfies 2022 Memoir/Autobiography Category goes to..."

Please let it be me.

It wasn't me. I sank down in my seat, embarrassed to have failed.

Just this once I wanted to be good at something. Despite my new-found confidence, I still wanted to show Mum and everyone else that all this meant something. *That I meant something.*

I didn't linger after the ceremony, knowing I had to catch a bus and tube back to the coach station to get the coach home and conscious that I really had no idea where I was going.

Once I safely got back to Victoria station, the effects of the day hit me – the disappointment of not winning, the stress of getting lost. Hungry, tired and flat, I headed to the station cafés, three of them, and began a binge that would last the entire journey home: a cheese baguette, four doughnuts, two cakes, an almond pastry and a chocolate bar for the coach.

I stepped off the final bus just after 11pm and went straight into the late-night off-licence. One bag of chocolate buttons and toffee popcorn later, it was done.

WHO IS SHE?

MAY 2022

Ding!

My laptop alerts me to a notification in our work group chat. I've been tagged in an image.

My heart begins to race. Oh please, *no*.

I click on the notification.

There is a photo of a middle-aged woman. Who is she? That *isn't* me. I can't possibly look like that. There is no way I could be that ... that ... big. That old. That middle-aged.

You're so vain.

"Wow, Emily, love the hair!"

"So good to see your face again, Emily."

My colleagues begin to leave comments but I can't read a thing. My cheeks are burning red and tears are running down my face.

I stand up and push my chair back and run to the toilet. I have to escape that photo, now.

You are so fat, Emily. Old and fat and now everyone has seen you.

A couple of weeks after the London Book Fair, an opportunity had come up at work to spend the afternoon at a local school doing some outreach work. I volunteered because it was my old secondary school. I had last been there thirty-five years earlier and I was curious to see how much it had changed.

My team at work had been home-based for over two years so it meant I hadn't seen anyone in person for much of that time. I'd been struggling with binge-eating disorder throughout that period and my weight had fluctuated. I was now at my heaviest weight ever and a little nervous of what the other staff would think of my new size. The last time I had seen them, I was three stones lighter, yet as much as I was self-conscious of my weight change, I didn't really know what I looked like. Apart from a brief glance in a changing room a couple of weeks earlier, I never looked at myself in a full-length mirror. I'd hidden the one at home over a year earlier. All I had was shaving mirrors in the bathroom and a small mirror in the loft – the kind that shows you from the neck up.

I didn't see myself the way others did. When you have lived with a vindictive troll in your head telling you your weight means everything, not looking in a full-length mirror is an act of self-preservation.

I greeted my colleague with a warm embrace, holding her dearly as you would a long-lost friend. Of course, she didn't care I'd gained weight and even if she did notice and quietly thought the same, she was right. I *had* gained three stones but was I any less of the person she remembered?

Before we began our presentation, I asked to use the bathroom and the head teacher showed me to the staff toilets. Entering the building felt strange, yet familiar. I shuddered.

She led me past the gym – the one I used to stand in. The large windows with their oversized black fabric curtains remained unchanged. I'd stood there all those years ago, at the back of the hall hoping someone would pick me first for their sports team, but they never did. I was a consolation teammate, me and my two left feet – always in the bottom two.

I passed the changing rooms – the ones I used to change uncomfortably in after sports and hope Miss would let us off from showering in front of each other. I hated the shape of my body back then. I still did.

I saw snippets of another life and could feel the energy of those memories running uncomfortably through my body. Suddenly I was twelve years old again and I wanted to cry.

"I used to go to this school!" I blurted out.

She smiled. "Really, I suppose it's changed a lot since you left?"

"May I take a quick look?" I asked.

"Of course." She pointed, leading the way.

The assembly hall was unaltered with the same large wooden stage at one end – a place I feared. I'd hide at the back of it when it was my class' turn to perform. The oak parquetry floor remained intact though well-worn and sloping in places. I wondered how many girls' feet had fallen across that floor over the years.

I wished the school had been empty – I longed to walk the lengthy corridors, run my hands along the walls and touch my memories once again. I wanted to do it all again, but differently this time. A melancholic nostalgia washed over me. Where had my life gone?

I headed to the staff toilet then back out to the carpark to meet up with my colleagues. Before we finished our outreach afternoon, the head teacher asked for a picture of us all for their noticeboard and so we stood behind their makeshift workstation and I grinned uncomfortably.

"*Cheese!*" we sang in unison.

Please hurry up and take the picture because I'm dying inside here, I thought.

I'd left that school at fifteen years old, anorexic and uncertain about life. I'd stood in that very spot thirty-five years earlier and cried because I was leaving my friends and the school that offered stability and routine at a time when nothing else in my life did. Now I was back and I didn't recognise the new version of me: old, overweight and grimacing. The expression on my face in the photo showed exactly how I had felt at the time.

It really unsettled me, but what upset me the most was *why* it made me feel that way. How could I be so vain? Why did I care so much about how I appeared to the world? Because for thirty-seven years I'd cared way too much about food and diets and my body shape. There were times in my life I honestly wished I could have sewn my mouth together so I couldn't eat. There were times when I wanted to be hospitalised and have food withdrawn from me just so I had a break from the constant obsessive thoughts about it. A coma would stop it all. And I would lose weight.

So I did what I do best: I vowed to stop eating again. Diet number 147,621.

By day two of the diet, I was back at it; back to the binge. Where was the willpower of my teens to withhold food? Why couldn't I do that again? If being overweight made me *that* unhappy, why couldn't I just stop overeating?

A couple of days later, I was getting out of the shower and noticed some purple marks on my hip and my heart sunk. They were fresh stretch marks, my first ones in twenty-one years. The last ones had been legitimised by carrying another human being inside me. These ones had no such justification. These were a gift of my constant gluttony.

I walked the dog, silently planning a new resolution to starve myself for the next week or two. I would eat fruit, soup and not much more. The voice of reason popped in reminding me that starving wouldn't work, it would just fuel the cycle, but my troll interrupted it: *Losing a stone would feel so good, Emily. Being thinner will make you feel happier!*

HORMONAL SWINGS

MAY 2022

I RECEIVED A NOTIFICATION FROM THE LOCAL HOSPITAL: I'D reached the top of the eighteen-month waiting list for two surgical procedures I had been waiting on and both were scheduled two weeks' apart. It would mean yet more time off work and the second operation – to remove a bunion on my right foot – would take me off my feet for at least six weeks.

In the lead up to the surgery, I began to binge once again. I thought it was the stress of the impending surgery but somehow it felt different. This time, I could not satiate my desire for carbs and sugar, eating just two things: bread and sweets. But this felt different to my previous binges. Usually, the foods were preplanned and consumed in a one-to-two-hour window at night with a whole buffet of forbidden treats. Instead, I was grazing all day long on bread and anything sweet. Some days I was consuming 4–5,000 calories easily.

The bingeing lasted ten days straight and as a result I was distressed, uncomfortable, bloated and very emotional. I was snapping at Jack, Thomas, the dog – anyone who strayed near me and irritated me even slightly.

I got up one evening from my desk in the kitchen and

headed to the bathroom and as I moved, I felt an unfamiliar warmth between my legs. Blood. It was my first period in almost twelve years and the heaviest I have ever experienced.

A few days later I went to the hospital for my pre-op assessment and the nurse routinely asked me for the date of my last period.

I smiled. "It was last Friday, actually. My first in many years."

The nurse stopped writing and looked up at me. "It's best if you get that checked with your GP. Its uncommon to get a period after so many years."

The period lasted a week and its arrival, although a huge surprise, brought a very welcome side-effect along with it: I had zero cravings for sugar or carbohydrates, in fact I hadn't even thought about food. I had been taking the inositol supplement that the homeopathic doctor had prescribed for almost five months and I was sure it had helped to level out my hormones, thus causing my period.

A couple of days later, I saw my GP and as she typed notes on her computer for my impending blood tests. I told her about the period and complete cessation of desire to binge.

"You don't think your bingeing is partly hormonal, do you?" she gasped, turning from her computer to look at me.

I knew I had an eating disorder and I knew I ate for comfort too, but I was beginning to wonder about the possible connection between my hormones and the recent all-day bingeing episodes. Maybe it was just a coincidence.

For the following two weeks I ate normally; no planning, no dieting, no restriction or bingeing. I had zero cravings but the most liberating thing was, I didn't notice it at the time. My head was free from its constant obsession with food. I can't begin to describe the sense of freedom I felt during that time; it moved me to tears when I realised how much time my thoughts of diet, food and bingeing had been consuming me.

The following week, I went into hospital for the first operation. Two of my four wisdom teeth were impacted and one was sitting particularly close to the sinus cavity – the surgeon chose to remove it under a general anaesthetic. It was a swift procedure carried out as a day-patient and I was home by late afternoon, a little sore and with stitches and a numb jaw. I couldn't open my mouth a great deal and was groggy from the anaesthetic. Yet the first thing I did when I got home was head for the kitchen. I needed comfort. I buttered bread and sucked it through my front teeth then I pulped a blueberry muffin with my mouth and painfully swallowed it down past the holes in my jaw.

Despite the discomfort and salty mouthwashes, the risk of trapped food, the bingeing intensified at night and continued once more, but then it changed and began to last all day. Not even intense jaw pain from oral surgery could stop me from doing this to myself.

About ten days later my surgical wounds had healed and the bingeing stopped. Later that day, my second period in almost twelve years arrived, almost five weeks after the first. This was no coincidence and I needed to find the connection.

I was forty-six years old when I started binge-eating and it had ebbed and flowed for four years. During that time, my life was incredibly challenging and self-care was a distant memory, so I missed some of the classic red flags of perimenopause. I'd experienced them all: stronger body odour, dry, thinning skin and regular and unexpected incontinence. Plucking my chin of its black whiskers had become a regular part of my new beauty routine, along with my nipples.

No one had ever warned me about this slide towards middle

age. It felt like as I was approaching fifty years old, everything was either falling out, leaking, thinning or sprouting growth in unwanted places. But all these little annoyances, along with the recent all-day binges, had one thing in common – they were all potentially symptoms of low oestrogen levels, something I discovered through a simple online search. And it wasn't until I got my first period in over a decade that I realised it. I needed to validate my findings with the doctor.

The doctor arranged for me to have some blood tests and week or so later I had my results back. They had come back '*normal – no further action required*' but I wanted to know what that meant to me. What was normal?

My doctor called and confirmed the bloods had shown I was in the middle of a normal menstrual cycle, a result that confirmed the timing since my last period. It seemed that my perimenopause had paused somehow and my doctor was a little baffled. Stress and lack of sleep can affect the body's ability to balance hormones and both had been major factors in my life for several years but finally things had eased in the previous few months. Could my body have been returning to a more balanced state as my environment at home was improving? Perhaps the inositol had also contributed to levelling my hormones out – my doctor googled it whilst on the phone, fascinated by what she found, but even more interested that I could see a couple of my recent all-day bingeing episodes coinciding with the return of my periods. I discovered some scientific research that showed a link between hormone deficiency and overeating. In some people this could lead to binge-eating episodes.

My doctor advised that my hormones would continue to fluctuate given my age and so at some point in the future, I could consider hormone replacement therapy (HRT). But for now she wanted me to continue to take the inositol. It felt amazing for my own doctor to acknowledge that an alternative supplement could quite possibly be a contributory factor in helping to balance my low oestrogen levels, along with regular sleep, a little more self-care and the improvement in my home environment. It felt amazing to just be heard.

TAKE AWAY THE PAIN

JUNE 2022

It was time for operation number two, the one on my foot that I had been dreading. It wasn't so much the surgery itself – I was a little naive about that – but the six-week recovery that would see me off my feet for a minimum of four weeks. It was under local anaesthetic and although I was protected by a sheet so I couldn't see anything, I was still having bones broken and removed and my toe pinned whilst awake in a bright white surgical theatre. There was no pain, but I felt everything.

It was mid-way through the operation when the surgeon began using a bone-cutting tool, I experienced my first panic attack ever. I had a nurse either side of me, holding my hands, soothing me in an attempt to keep me calm. Although I didn't feel any pain, I could feel the vibration running through my body as the bone was being cut away and that combined with the shrill sound, not unlike a dentist drill, terrified me. I couldn't control this situation – someone had taken it away from me. I began to panic; my heart was racing.

"I can't do this. I can't breathe!" I searched from one nurse's eyes to the other, desperately.

"It's okay, Emily, you are doing brilliantly, just take some deep breaths," one soothed.

"I don't like it, I don't think I can do it."

I want my mum.

"Just breathe, that's it. Nice and slowly, Emily."

When the bone-cutting stopped, I calmed down a little.

"Now, Miss Johnson, I want you to sit up and take a look at your foot before I bandage it, as it won't look like this the next time you see it," my surgeon said encouragingly.

Underneath the iodine streaks, my foot was ghostly pale from the tourniquet still tightly tied around my ankle stopping the blood flow. It didn't look like my foot at all. A large four-inch cut was sewn neatly together.

I wanted to cry. It had felt like the longest forty-five minutes of my life and probably the most mentally and physically traumatising. I wasn't prepared for the surgery, nor the pain afterwards and loss of mobility. Being unable to walk made me feel vulnerable and that vulnerability made me weak in my own eyes.

A couple of hours after the surgery, I was wheeled to Paul who was waiting in the hospital carpark. We were still separated, by life and circumstance, but this man was my rock when I needed help. And right then, I needed my rock.

As the nurse waved me off into Paul's care, I burst into tears recounting the operation to him. He soothed me gently with a love and kindness I rarely allowed others to show me.

I was sent home with painkillers and a bandaged foot in a boot, still numb with the local anaesthetic. The pain was bearable at first, but as the anaesthetic wore off and the bone and nerve pain kicked in, the reality hit me. I couldn't move or walk unaided – for the first time in years, I couldn't manage a situation alone.

I'd booked myself into a budget hotel after the surgery

under the illusion that I could watch television and relax for two days. It meant I could avoid all the flights of stairs in and outside our flat. But it was no holiday. I couldn't stand up at all. I crawled to the bathroom on my hands and knees and Paul had to lift me onto the toilet.

I remember sitting on the toilet, holding onto the towel rail for balance, staring at Paul as I cried in both pain and embarrassment. I'd never felt so vulnerable or dropped my guard down low enough to allow anyone to help me with something so personal. I had to let him close to me; I had no choice but allow him to help me.

Outwardly, I have always been fiercely independent. I've worn my independence as a badge of honour. It was just the way it had been since I was seventeen and both my parents left the country. I never asked anyone for help, I preferred doing things myself. It was just easier that way.

In eight years of knowing him, Paul had never rescued me – I'd never allowed him to – but there I sat, crying and peeing in front of a man I still loved, looking at the helplessness in his eyes watching the woman he still loved, in pain.

Is that love? It's a moment I will never forget. To be held up, to be quietly loved in our lowest, most vulnerable human moments. It felt like love and it drew us closer together once again.

The painkillers sickened my stomach and the first couple of days were spent in a fog of medication-induced sleep with Paul checking in on me at the hotel. Two days later, I returned home to my sons who were pleased to see me and shocked by my immobility and obvious pain.

Once home, the need to binge returned, once more for comfort. After my first dressing change a week after the surgery, I saw my foot for the first time, battered, heavily bruised and sewn together – Frankenstein's foot. Just the nurse touching it brought it all back – suddenly I was back in the theatre with that noise, that feeling. Reliving the trauma. I began to cry silently.

The shock sickened me, but when I left the hospital the first thing I did was hobble to the café opposite for the biggest, sweetest slice of red velvet cake. I sat there quietly crying, eating my cake. It didn't even taste that great, it was dry around the edges from being under the cabinet lights for too long. But that didn't stop me eating it all. I could at least see now that I was eating for comfort.

About ten days after the surgery, the need to binge was growing and I needed to see if I could walk a few more steps than just to the toilet and back. I gingerly left the flat, sliding down the stairs on my backside to the front door. Armed with a borrowed walking stick and determination, I headed slowly down the hill. It was very steep and it wasn't long before I realised I'd made a mistake. There was no way my foot was ready for walking several metres and I really needed to get back home, but I didn't even know if I could turn around.

At the bottom of the hill, about ten metres away, was a betting shop. A man was standing outside it watching me – a staff member having a quick smoke. He stubbed out his cigarette and extended his hand to me. "Here love, take my hand – let me help you down." He smiled, kindness in his face.

Without hesitation, I placed my hand in his. "Thank you," I replied gratefully.

His hand was warm. I felt safe as he led me down the hill to the flat pavement.

"Thank you so much." I smiled, fighting back the tears, hating that I needed to be helped, but touched that a stranger had offered.

As I walked a couple more metres I stopped – I could not continue and it had been foolish to think I could have walked alone. I turned and slowly made my way back home up the hill alone and empty-handed. My mission to get my usual binge foods had been thwarted and that made the craving, now fuelled with anger and desperation, even more intense.

A few days later, I needed more painkillers and the urge to binge was overwhelming. I wanted to try and walk again and this time I was even more determined. I managed a little further – almost to my nearest supermarket – but by then the pain overwhelmed me and I sat on the wall by the bus stop – the one I'd often sit and eat my doughnuts on – and I cried once again. I felt angry with myself. *Get on with it, stop moaning,* I said to myself. *You're stronger than this.*

I stood up, using the stick to steady myself and managed a few more metres, before stopping once again.

"Come, place your arm on mine. Where are you going?"

I feel a firm grip hold my arm up and turn to see a young woman, no more than twenty-five or so with almost-white, blonde hair. She is clutching a stuffed white teddy bear – something that strikes me as odd. My angel is an alcoholic, a street drinker – the pungent smell of booze surrounds her entirely. She must have been sitting with a group of the regular drinkers and seen me struggling to walk.

"Oh ... um thank you. I'm going in there," I mumble in embarrassment, pointing at the supermarket.

The angel gently turns me towards her and looks me in the eyes as she holds my arm firmly. "Come, let me help you. You do know how well you are doing, don't you? Please, keep going."

She leads me to the door of the supermarket and then she turns round and disappears.

HEALING, FINALLY

JULY-AUGUST 2022

A couple of weeks passed and it was time for my next therapy session with Stacey – this time it would be Advanced Conversational Hypnosis (ACH). We'd scheduled it for 6am from the comfort of my bed. That way, I knew the house would be peaceful and I could completely surrender to the experience. I trusted Stacey implicitly and was willing to try anything to curb the bingeing. I was desperate to heal my relationship with food, but more importantly to heal my relationship with myself.

ACH is quite different to other forms of hypnosis. Rather than lying flat and slowly going into a trance, I began my session sitting up, eyes open and aware of my surroundings. Although much of what happened remains slightly blurred (I had a later discussion with Stacey to enable me to write this section in more detail) I was under hypnosis and experiencing periods of deep trance. During the session, a couple of things were revealed by my subconscious mind which have had a profound effect on my journey to loving and accepting myself.

We began preparations for my session by speaking openly about my recent surgery and how I had struggled to be vulnerable and to let others help me; how I'd labelled myself as weak for not tolerating the pain and immobility better. I told her about how Paul had helped me onto the toilet, how the man at the betting shop had given me his hand, how neighbours had brought me food and how hard I had found it to accept their help.

"How do you feel when people offer to help you, Emily?" Stacey questioned gently.

"I don't like it. I don't want their help, because I am strong. I've had to be since I was seventeen. I don't need anyone's help, I can manage..." I trailed off.

"When you help others, Emily – your friends, your neighbours, people on the street – do you see them as weak for needing your help?" Stacey enquired.

"No ... I just see them as needing help," I answered, puzzled. "And how does it make you feel when you can help those people?"

"It makes me feel useful, happy I can do something and make things easier for them somehow."

"So do you believe they think you are weak when you need help?" she continued.

"No," I replied.

"And how do you think it makes others feel when they can help you?" Stacey enquired.

"Maybe it makes them happy they were able to help me?"

"That's right, Emily. You've been strong since you were a teenager and you have put a wall up. You felt no one was there for you but you, so you depended only on you and that way you couldn't be disappointed. You are not weak, you are human and sometimes we need to ask others for help and that's okay. Don't deny someone the gift of helping you, Emily."

I'd never framed it that way before. It made me feel good to help others. It was a natural human response to reach out and help them times of need. It's what we do. It's what we are meant to do. Why should I prevent others from having that same opportunity?

Now more relaxed and feeling comfortable, it was time to begin the session.

"What's the problem?" Stacey began.

"I want to stop binge-eating," I answered.

"You want to stop binge-eating," Stacey repeated.

Yes, I want to stop bingeing," I echoed.

"How does binge-eating impact your life?"

"I hate it. It affects everything. Food is all I think about."

"Tell me about your relationship with food."

"I had anorexia when I was thirteen and now I have a problem with binge-eating chocolate, cakes, bread and doughnuts. I just don't understand it."

"Tell me about when you began to restrict food when you were thirteen, Emily. What was happening in your life at the time – can you tell me?" Stacey spoke softly, soothingly.

"Um ... I used to go to an all-girls' school and I wanted to fit in with the other girls. I was shorter than my two best friends ... and fatter. I wanted to be like them... I wanted to be slimmer. My dad left then too. He didn't really care about me... Not eating made me feel in control."

"It made you feel in control?"

"Yes, it did."

"Tell me about that need to feel in control, Emily. In what way was controlling food going to make a difference?"

"All I had was to control my food, my body."

"How did it help you?"

I began to cry. "It didn't help me, but it was all I had. I've been trying to have control ever since." I covered my face as I sobbed.

"That's right, let it out..." Stacey said, pausing between each encouraging statement. "Tears are good... Get it all... All the way."

I settled once more.

"You found yourself in a new world as a teenager, Emily, one that you had no say over. Everything was suddenly different. You felt alone and wanted acceptance and validation, but you didn't realise your validation could only come from you. You are free to love you now, Emily.

"Tell me how you feel when you eat chocolate, or cake, or those doughnuts, Emily," Stacey gently enquired.

I looked around the room. "Excitement beforehand, I guess. Pleasure and comfort, momentarily. But out-of-control, shame. Disgust. I hate myself afterwards."

"Tell me more about the comfort you feel from food when you binge. What does that comfort feel like to you?"

I sighed and felt my eyes closing as I slipped deeper into hypnosis. "Um... It feels like ... like ... like ... a ... hug," I cried.

"I know," Stacey soothed, before pausing. "A hug – it feels like a hug," she repeated.

I began to sob once more.

"That's right, let it out... Great job... Tears are good... All the way," Stacey said softly, pausing between each statement.

Whilst Stacey continued to explore with me the comforting elements I'd found in food, without noticing at first, I found myself gently stroking my thigh, caressing my leg tenderly the way in which I had stroked my sons' temples as babies to soothe them. As I was speaking to Stacey, I was aware of the warm sensation of my fingers on my bare skin and how comforting it felt to me, over and over in soft, delicate strokes.

My unconscious mind had released the beliefs that had kept

me from loving myself and without any conscious awareness, I responded by gently soothing myself. At last, I was showing myself the same love I'd been showing others my whole life.

I can remember Stacey asking me to see a table before me filled with my favourite binge foods: chocolate, doughnuts, cakes – everything I could imagine – and asking me if I wanted to eat them now.

I shook my head. "No, I don't need to," I whispered.

Two hours had slipped past – I stopped crying and opened my eyes.

I'm standing on the high street opposite a supermarket, just staring. They sell cakes, doughnuts, biscuits, bread here – all those things *used* to be my top tier in binge foods. Paul is sitting in the car waiting for me.

I just stand and stare.

There is silence. Not a word is spoken. Not a sound.

Just the noise of traffic driving by. People chatting. Children laughing.

I need to test the urge to binge. Could this *really* be gone?

I find myself inside already, in the bakery aisle, looking at the blueberry muffins, the coconut raspberry cake, the baguettes and biscuits and trays of doughnuts in rows. I could buy them all, but I don't need to today. Not now. Not anymore. Where has that woman gone? Tears appear and I can't stop them.

One by one, I'm scanning my items through the self-check-out: orange juice, sliced turkey, bananas and a loaf of bread.

There is no need to rush this time. Paul is waiting for me. His eyes meet mine and he smiles.

I crumple and begin to sob.

"What's wrong, Emily? Please don't cry." He pulls me into

his arms and his warmth and the familiarity of his skin dissolves me.

"I don't know. I just feel so sad," I manage to say in between sobs.

"Shh, it's okay my darling, I've got you." Paul's fingertips touch my tears and he gently wipes them away. This time I let him hold me. This time, I let him in.

"Thanks for the lift, Paul," I call out, waving goodbye. I'm not lingering to chat today; there is something I need to do.

Later that day I go upstairs to the mirror on the landing wall. The one that's been hidden behind the wooden unit and boxes, with the piles of clothes on top I can no longer fit into. I push them all to one side.

It's time.

I stare at myself. My long brown hair falls over my shoulders and down my back. Grey wispy curls frame my face. I look at my teeth, slightly yellowed and worn.

My face is round. Yes, it is. It *is* round.

I'm wearing a white cotton T-shirt and black leggings up to my waist.

I look at my arms and trace the shape of my legs through my leggings. They are arms and legs. Yes, that's what they are.

I turn to the side, following the curve of my breasts down, over the rolls of flesh underneath them – one roll, two rolls – and settle my sight on my belly. Yes, it *is* round.

I hold my belly. My beautiful, round belly.

I'm staring at my reflection now. There isn't a sound.

Just one voice.

My voice.

"I fucking love you, Emily."

After that early morning ACH therapy session, everything changed. I ate a piece of coffee cake for breakfast that morning – just one slice, not four. It was delicious, but it was just cake. There was no guilt this time, no spitting it out, calorie-counting or thoughts of regret. I enjoyed every sweet, buttery mouthful. I hadn't broken any diets, I hadn't sinned – I'd just eaten a slice of cake at breakfast time.

I didn't binge at night again. I felt no need to and there were no more urges after my session. In the beginning I was scared that the feeling wouldn't last, that perhaps it was only temporary. Suddenly I had all this room in my head that used to be filled with thoughts of food, of calories and weighing scales and a hatred for my body. But those were all gone, released somehow – healed.

EPILOGUE

I'M LYING ALONE IN THE DARKNESS OF THE LOFT SPACE. IT'S my fiftieth birthday. Something washes over me: a realisation.

Ageing is a privilege, not a luxury afforded to everyone, as my dad had discovered. I've reached the decade my dad passed away in, a life incomplete. He died with many things left to do, places to go and wounds to heal. Some of the friends I went to school with are already dead and buried through one tragedy or another. How lucky I am to have reached this milestone: fifty years on this planet.

I may have thirty years left of this experience we call life if I'm very lucky. Maybe I have three months, who knows, but either way I can't control when that time may be. I can only do my best to look after this body of mine.

I've spent years worrying about trivial things, insignificant things, half of which have never happened, yet I've sacrificed so much precious time and energy worrying needlessly. Way bigger challenges have come along, ones I never saw coming, and I overcame them all, every single one.

Something else occurs to me as I lie here in the darkness – this skin and these bones have held my life for fifty years and have served me well. I've carried three children and birthed two. That alone is a miracle. I've touched, seen, heard, smelt and tasted; I've experienced *life*. I've loved hard and I've laughed. I've *really* hurt too. I have felt every human emotion possible during that time and I have survived them all. I've memories that I hope will stay forever and some I'd rather forget, but have found peace with nonetheless.

But as I lie in those final moments of my life, will I *really* be wishing I'd fitted into the next dress size down or that my arms were more toned or belly flatter? Will I wish for fewer wrinkles or my dark brown curls back? Or will I wish I had more time with my precious sons, my grandchildren if they come along, with Paul? Will I wish I looked up at the stars more or stopped long enough in my day to watch the clouds roll by like I did as a child? That I sat and enjoyed a slice of cake, or maybe two, with a best friend over a coffee? Or will I really be worried that my bum looked big in my leggings back in 2022?

How will people really remember me after I'm gone? Will they think of me as that woman who carried a few extra pounds or will I be remembered for the way I loved them, the way I cared for everyone I encountered in my life.

Now I have my answer.

AFTERWORD

Since the age of thirteen I have been on every diet possible. I was no happier with my body shape at six and a half stones, then I was at thirteen and half stones. It was never really about my actual weight – the absence of happiness came from deep within. I pinned my value to myself and others inextricably on my weight. Everything depended on it; being liked, loved, accepted, needed. I believed my weight was what people saw in me first, how they judged me. It was really just a lack of self-love and acceptance but to me, it was *always* about my weight.

Many factors can contribute to the development of an eating disorder, not just a person's environment, or exposure to traumatic experiences, peer pressures and social media. Research has shown that eating disorders can run in families, suggesting that certain genes may make some people more vulnerable to developing an eating disorder or other related conditions such as depression, obsessive compulsive disorder and drug and alcohol addiction. Although undiagnosed, my dad displayed symptoms of disordered eating and excessive alcohol consumption. There is also a familial history of anxiety and depression on both sides of my family, as well as gambling addiction, obsessive compulsive disorder and alcoholism. It seems I may have carried those genes and sadly, passed them onto my children.

Aside from the genetic odds stacked against me, I now understand that my lifetime spent with disordered thoughts around food was in part due to being exposed as a child to my dad's own disordered relationship with food and his own appearance. I observed from a very young age how important body image was to my dad and so my young mind determined that my body shape would be important to him too; perhaps that's how he might have been judging me. The little time I spent with him, I was witness to his restrictive dieting and obsessive exercising to alter his body shape. I may have been just a small child but those memories stayed with me.

But more significantly, through therapy, I now recognise that my disordered relationship with food and myself was a symptom of not being seen or verified as a child by my dad. As adults we constantly read our environment and judge it by how we feel and see ourselves. As children, we judge it by our parents and our relationship with our caregivers. We are constantly looking for feedback on whether we are good enough. My dad's emotional distance whilst at home, was far more hurtful and damaging that his physical distance whilst working away.

My dad made me feel unnoticed and unimportant as a child. On some level, feeling unseen by him may have made me feel unloved and as a young child, I probably felt this was somehow my fault. So, veiled under the disguise of needing to diet, perhaps I starved myself as a form of self-punishment too, as well as a way to be seen.

I have struggled with relationships with men throughout my life. Therapy revealed the reasons why. I feared being rejected and abandoned again just as my dad had made me feel and so I clung on to each one. I needed them to love me at all costs and that turned me into a people-pleaser with very few boundaries.

I was invisible to the main man in my life as a child. It wasn't one moment that showed me that, but many: seeing paternal relationships on TV, watching my friends' fathers interact, hearing their stories or reading about relationships in books. Only then did I realise the relationship I had with my dad was different.

It's possible that on some level I thought that if I changed the way I looked it would please him and capture his attention. During this particularly vulnerable time in my life, TV adverts and magazines were reminding me constantly that thinner was better. Skinny was fashionable and beautiful. Women *should* be thin. It was coming at me from all angles and that's before the social-media bombardment we have today. Even back then, our worth was judged by our weight, our outward appearance. Those messages sunk in.

I believed my happiness and feelings of 'not good enough' were fixable if I fixed my weight. I have always had a tendency towards perfectionism and control since my teens. Being more than thin would trigger my perfectionism and diets would feed my need to control. When I began to receive attention through the anorexia, it reminded me that people really did care. It taught me that food, or at least the act of withholding it, could get me love.

Perhaps on an unconscious level, I just wanted my parents' attention and the eating disorder certainly got my mum's. Sadly, it didn't get my dad's. It was probably his recognition I needed the most, but he was in his own world, on the other side of mine at the time.

Food became my language of love throughout my life. Whether working around food, cooking for others, feeding the homeless on the streets, or throwing dinner parties, food became my way of communicating love. It had also been my way of communicating pain. Withholding food became my cry for help during my anorexia days. It became my comfort blanket too when alone and in pain during my binge-eating days.

In the height of my bingeing, I was consuming thousands of calories in an evening, all of which was processed carbohydrates and sugar, neither offering my body any nutrition. I could easily consume over 300g of sugar in one sitting – far in excess of the daily recommended amount for an adult.

I was eating myself into ill health but felt powerless to stop it. Blood tests showed my liver was fatty and struggling, but I didn't need blood tests to tell me I didn't feel well. I was tired and lethargic. I often had heartburn and watery diarrhoea – a frequent aftermath of sustained binges.

At the time of writing this book, BED is the most common eating disorder in the United States (and the second most common in the UK) but nobody really knows about it. And nobody is really talking about it either. There are millions of Emilys out there, sadly – people just like me living with this eating disorder, or a different one, many unable to talk about it outside of the support groups. Some can't tell their families or partners or are unable to access help because of the shame they carry. Many try to get help, but they don't feel heard, or help is not available in their hometown. Covid has exacerbated waiting lists exponentially. I recently removed myself from the waiting list at my local eating-disorder clinic, I no longer feel I require their help. Despite the impact BED was having on my mental and physical health, I was on the waiting list for over eighteen months and had *still* not reached the top of the list in order to receive treatment. It's a healthcare lottery. It's not a choice to have an eating disorder. It's not a lack of willpower, or act of defiance, it's mental illness.

After my ACH session with Stacey, I was very emotional for a few weeks. It felt like grief and I didn't understand why. After the initial euphoria of being free of the binge-eating behaviours, there was relief and a little disbelief. Was this *really* over? But then an overwhelming sadness sank over me and I found myself crying outside supermarkets or staring at my former binge foods inside in floods of tears. I'd been dependent on a substance and whilst I don't like to compare food to addictive substances (it doesn't need any more negative connotations) at times my behaviour had been like Paul's when drinking or Thomas' when gambling. I'd lied. I'd borrowed money. I'd stolen food from people's plates. I'd eaten out of the bin to satiate that need.

Suddenly I didn't feel the need for that unhealthy support system. Like a former alcoholic walking past the off-licence that had been their 'go to' for months, years maybe, I could walk past cakes, biscuits, doughnuts and fresh bread and not feel compelled to buy them and it took some time to accept those feelings. I was grieving for a lost woman, a woman who had loathed her body and punished herself both with and without food and vile words; a woman who had never felt good enough, no matter how hard she had tried to be everyone's everything. Most of all, I was grieving for the time she'd lost hating herself along the way.

I've not returned to bingeing since my ACH therapy. I've lost weight, hardly surprising seeing as I'm no longer consuming thousands of additional calories a week. It doesn't matter how much weight I've lost. For the *first* time since the age of thirteen, it no longer matters.

Now I eat cake and chocolate and crisps and pastry and white bread; and everything else I banned or binged on, sometimes a little more than I need because I'm heading towards another period and I crave them insatiably. But now I feel free to eat them all. No guilt. There are no more food labels. No more good or bad foods. It's just food. No diets. No weighing scales. No self-hatred. No covering up mirrors or covering up me.

In August 2022 we enjoyed a warm summer spell and I didn't feel like spending another summer sweltering in leggings and oversized hoodies, ones that helped cover up my arms and tum. My half-century birthday revelation had really affected me and so had my hypnosis therapy. And so, as part of the shedding of the old me, I put on a beautiful summer dress, a sleeveless one, a maxi dress that had been banished to the bag in the loft of 'never wearing this out in public' outfits.

Paul took me to the local coffee shop – I was still recovering from foot surgery but determined as ever, I hobbled into the café and ordered my drink. I scouted the busy café. No one was looking at me, or more importantly, my arms or belly. They were way more concerned with their own real-life important matters.

I picked up my coffee and left. No one noticed. It wasn't so scary after all.

The next day it was my legs' turn. These pins have not had a grand public reveal in many years. Not brave enough to bare them fully, I put on some bronzer first, before pulling on knee-length shorts. Me, in shorts – who would have thought!

Paul drove me to the coffee shop and in I hobbled, my bare, corned-beef-fresh-out-of-a-can legs were on display. No one stared. No one really cared.

My limbs were finally liberated! And so, every day I dared to bare my arms and legs a little bit more over summer and every day, it got a little easier.

I will never have long, brown legs or svelte arms. Neither will I ever be eighteen again, or size eight. I've finally accepted that. The clothes in black bin bags have gone to a charity shop.

This is me. Gloriously, magnificently fifty-year-old me.

I just wish I had realised what a beautiful gift my body was a long time ago.

At the end of the summer, I received an email out of the blue from *HELLO!* Magazine. My dear friend, Lisa, had nominated me for a Star Mum Award as part of their annual Inspirational Awards. They were writing to let me know I had been short-listed to the final three. I was floored.

A few days later I popped into my local supermarket and spotted the latest magazine on the shelf. I flicked through it and there, along with celebrities and royals, was my picture. A finalist for a Star Mum award and I smiled through tears at a profound realisation. This was the same shop I had stood in for the last four years, telling myself how useless I was.

Fat, useless Emily.

Over and over. A failure of a mother, a wife, a co-worker, daughter, friend, and every bag of doughnuts and cakes and chocolate bars I bought in that same shop in preparation for a binge confirmed those feelings for me.

But now, I stood in the shop and someone wasn't telling me I was useless or fat or a failure, instead they were saying, in the loveliest possible way: *We see you, Emily and we think you are a star. Please see yourself the way others do.*

It was a voice far louder than my troll, one loud enough to shut it up. I smiled and I listened.

It didn't matter if I won the award or not. It was not about a title, it never was. The universe had a message for me and it was safely delivered.

Shortly before finishing this book, these words came to my mind whilst laying in the darkness one night. For anyone who may have stood in front of a mirror at some point in their lives and not loved the person looking back, I've written this for you. May you fall back in love with your reflection and remember each day how amazing you really are, in each and every way. With all my love, Emily x

The Mirror

Come, stand before me.
Please don't look away.
I came here, along with you all those years ago
But somehow you lost me along the way.
I know you want to run now
But please, this time, stay.

I've felt your pain and sorrow,
I've held your hand each day.
At times you shouted at me. You hated me.
You broke this heart that beats for you
But I loved you just the same.

You came here with promise, a gift to give the world
And one day, our journey will be over
But you'll always be remembered.
Not for these hips, this round belly, that gentle furrowed brow

But that smile, your presence,
The lives you touched through the hugs you held
And the warmth you gifted others through the
love you gave away.
I love you. I've always loved you.
I want nothing in return.
Just that you see yourself the way others do –
lovely in every way.

No need for tears now.
You've found me.
Welcome home, I've missed you.
Please, this time, stay.

November, 2022

A REQUEST FROM THE AUTHOR...

If you enjoyed *Belly*, please consider leaving a review on your chosen platform. It will help this book reach other people who need it, so that they know they're not alone.

Emily J. Johnson

ALSO BY EMILY J. JOHNSON

"...a story of survival against the odds ... how healing and hope are possible."

Eleanor Segall - author, mental-health blogger

Four years ago, Emily, a divorced mother of two, was living her best life with a new partner and blended family of six. But then addiction and mental illness entered her home uninvited, threatening to tear the whole family apart.

With an alcoholic husband and two teenage sons – one a depressed gambler and the other with chronic obsessive-compulsive disorder – Emily is left to cope alone. And when the Covid pandemic hits, she almost breaks too.

ACKNOWLEDGMENTS

I have been lucky enough during my lifetime to have some wonderful women walk me through some of the toughest times in my life, as well as the most joyful. I gift you my love and sincere thanks for holding my hand, both in person and across the miles and for keeping me afloat during the stormiest of seas. You are ALL remarkable women who have brought so much into my life and I will always be grateful for your friendship and love.

To Karen and Yvette for caring for me. To Ang for always standing beside me. To Sharon, Suzy J, Emma B, Suzette, Linda, Val, Sheila, Sue, Bridgette, Allison, Corinne, Deanna, Tammy and the rest of the Aussie crew – thank you.

To Laura O, Suzanne, Kristen, Nikki Lanzarote, Mrs F – you inspire me.

To the women I've connected with online – we've never met, but you lifted me up and inspired me without knowing.

To Naomi, Sonya, Emma, Niki, Becca, Penny, Molly, Aimee, Mila, Rebecca, Rachel – and the rest of my MOMs and team at work. My second family. Thank you for your incredible support, encouragement and fun!

To Ann, Christine and Amanda – thank you for the priceless memories.

To Clare B – thank you - you capture my visions for the book covers so beautifully.

To Lisa, my dear friend and editor who turned my books from scrambled thoughts to something worth publishing. Thank you for encouraging me and supporting me always. Because of you,

I'm an author. You gave me that belief in myself to write. Keep fanning the flames.

To Stella with angel's wings – keep shining, my little star. Thank you for always being there for me, my troll and I.

To Di, whom I've known since forever. You never fail to make me smile and light up my day.

To Stacey – The one who gave me the gift of healing my wounds. Forever my soul sister.

To Mum, the woman who gave me everything – you are the best mum any daughter could hope for and I will love you always and forever, until the end of time.

ABOUT THE AUTHOR

Emily J. Johnson is a mother, author and advocate for raising awareness and improving access to mental-health services. Having spent fifteen years living in Western Australia, Emily returned to the UK in 2010 and now lives on the south coast of England with her two sons and Billy – the family dog.

Emily continues to live and work around her family's ongoing mental illness whilst splitting her time between part-time work, full-time caring and any-time writing, whenever possible.

Printed in Great Britain
by Amazon

20337743R00154